The
CHEAT CODE
It's Only 1 Code

by Lonnie Harrell

The Cheat Code

TABLE OF CONTENTS

INTRO

DEVELOPMENT IS A process, and that process varies greatly from individual to individual. Who, at birth, knows how tall they will be or what body-type they will have? And who among us could have predicted all of the physical, social, economic, and mental influences that would flow into our lives similar to the way a storm blows from the sea onto land; sometimes unexpected but every time inevitable?Like many events in our lives, the process of skill development has unforeseen challenges and accompanying changes beyond our control. Pastor John C. Maxwell wrote, "Change is inevitable. Growth is optional".By that rationale, the determination of which actions are most appropriate in the face of adversity are exclusive to the individual who experiences the adversity. Development, specifically player development, is determined by effort. Effort is determined by mindset. Despite the changing and challenging landscapes associated with player development, the player has complete control over their mindset. Thus, the player controls how they react to adversity and ultimately how they develop. This book has been written for all of the coaches, players, parents and for the basketball community that hungers for specific answers to player development. It has been said that success manifests itself most clearly at the intersections of preparation and opportunity.Seasoned with highs and lows, achievements and trials, moments of accomplishment and instances of failure; the ingredients

that make up the recipe for preparation can be daunting. Despite the waves of adversity that powerfully beat against the rocks of doubt and fear within the human mind, invaluable life lessons are to be learned and character is to be built from those waves. For the young men and women who participate in sports there is a new voice of wise counsel. Lonnie "L- Train" Harrell aka "Prime Objective," has an unmatched passion for youth sports development. A native of Washington, D.C., he began playing basketball as a child. He later went on to compete at both collegiate and professional levels. A combination of Lonnie's basketball history along with his infectious personality have provided him with an audience to some of basketball's most respected and revered players, analysts, coaches, administrators, and owners. He has sat at feet of basketball greatness and has soaked up every drop of insight and wisdom for the sole

purpose of sharing the lessons with those who fall under the span of his influence. By writing this book, Lonnie attempts to broaden the view of every reader as it pertains to youth skill development. Through stories of his own encounters and experiences, Lonnie unravels a scroll as entertaining as it is wise. In highlighting events and interactions with renowned men and women of basketball throughout the country, this book offers personal insight from a variety of sources to assist the reader in understanding the most proven practices in player development. Within the following pages are stories worth reading, examples worth emulating and counsel worth accepting; hopefully for generations to come. If experience is the best educator then hopefully, the culmination of thoughts and in-

sight as well as the advice given through the personal experiences revealed within these pages will offer the reader decades of wisdom and create The Cheat Code.

DEDICATION

To: Naomi Brooks, My Grandmother and biggest fan. You have created a beautiful and strong family and I'm thankful for the man that I have become because of the foundation you have built. Growing up in a home with 5 women of different generations, being the youngest and having an uncle that taught me how to be a protector, is why I serve God daily to armor myself with the strength necessary to lead and protect. Thank you for your love and guidance.

To: Raymond Euell, My uncle (earth Father) and best life coach. You taught me about everything. It was nothing I couldn't come to you to learn. You were my everything. Continue to be my guidance and my guardian Angel. Thank you for teaching me survival and how to be a competitor. You were way before your time and you put me years beyond mine. Heaven has a good one.

To: All...

...of the people who have supported me and been there for me and never wavered. To the families who trusted me and allowed me to be a part of their kids' futures. To the ones who witnessed it, and refused to appreciate it. All of the players i have ever competed against, and with, to everyone who told me NO, and lacked faith, I thank you. Because of all of you, this gem is full of all of those experiences and so much more. You all fueled this, and gave me more reason to study the game and make it MINE!

KOBE BRYANT

I WAS THE recipient of passes in one of the best games in Rucker Park history in 2002 in Harlem, New York, that would go viral online. None other than Kobe Bryant, a five-time NBA champion with three rings at the time, made those passes. When I looked back and watched the old video of the game, I saw how well-matched our playing was considering it was our first time playing together.

My squad, Murda Inc, was coached by Irv Gotti, Chris Gotti, and Ja Rule when I was competing in the EBC (Entertainers Basketball Classic) at Rucker Park. I was introduced to the Rucker by Ellis and Todd (Short Man), two of my guys. At the time, Murda Inc. was the most well-known and hottest record label, and I was the franchise player for them. Except for our team, most teams in the league had several NBA players on their roster. For the biggest games, we occasionally had special NBA guests fly in to match the others. Fat Joe's Terror Squad used to provide the muscle, so we had to refresh our roster with more talent. Two NBA players would come off the bench and three NBA players would start for Fat Joe. Queens residents of different skill levels made up my team.

Irv and Steve Stoute arranged for Kobe to play at Rucker Park because he had always wanted to. To boost his street cred and play with me, they invited Kobe to Harlem. I spent one day of my life playing with probably the best backcourt Rucker Park has ever seen! A new phase in history had started.

Being the competitor that I am, I wanted to play against Kobe when I learned that he was coming to play with me. I am a Lakers fan, but before Kobe, I was an Iverson supporter. Iverson is a Hall of Fame player and a friend. We played together a few times and were very dangerous as teammates. At the time, I chose Iverson over Kobe as my favorite player. The other players believed Kobe was the best, and I've always wanted to play against the best and in 1996, a discussion happened that fueled my fire even more. I was playing for the Orlando Magic in a pre-season game, and Allen Iverson and I were in the hotel lobby talking basketball and joking about who could grow their hair the fastest because we both had small fro's. In that discussion, he had told one of his teammates how good of a player I was and that he would choose me over anybody. That did a lot for my confidence and ego.

That same year, Shaq had already decided to leave Orlando and join the Lakers after the draft and before the start of the season. I was living with former Magic star, Dennis Scott at the time in his Isleworth, Florida house while he was a member of the Magic. He advised me to preserve my money because his home is spacious. When I started with the Magic, I was staying in a hotel; after that, I moved in with Dennis.

Isleworth, a posh neighborhood in Orlando, was at the time the most popular Florida neighborhood for celebrities. Shaq, Ken Griffey Jr., Bill Gates, Penny Hardaway, Tiger Woods, and others called it home. In this gated community with lakes and golf courses, I saw these guys every day touring the neighborhood on their boats or golf carts. One morning as we were eating breakfast before working out, Shaq entered the room. Since he and Dennis were like brothers, he never knocks and enters immediately. He adds, "I'm gone," as he walks into the kitchen.He goes on, "I'm going to LA," and Dennis and I exchange shocked looks. Jerry West, known as "The Logo," promised to look after me and said that the little lad he had acquired, Kobe, would help bring championships to Los Angeles.We will establish a dynasty. We were in shock. Nobody anticipated Shaq leaving Orlando, since it was his City.

Shaq stared at me after telling me about his plan to switch teams and remarked, "Kobe will bust your ass." Dennis spoke out right away to defend me, so I was able to react with a laugh. They were arguing over who among myself and this youngster named Kobe was the best. I recalled that discussion and how much I yearned to compete against him. Six years later, the investigative part of me was still curious about who was truly the best. I'm grateful it never occurred and that it didn't happen at that time. The result far outweighed any bragging rights each of us might have had. The experience of playing together turned out to be legendary.

The hype had been built up before the game. As one of the season's hottest players, Hot 97 radio station in New York consistently supported me and advertised my games in the park. But on this particular day, social media wasn't as prevalent back then as it is now, so everyone in New York City knew that Kobe was coming. By way of the radio station and word-of-mouth in the streets, the information spread. At the time, Murda Inc. was the trendiest label, and when you're hot, word spreads quickly.

I arrived at the Park early to experience the thrill because I was a big fan of the game. People were gathered in their apartment windows, on bridges, rooftops, and atop fences to catch a sight of the park and lines that extended down the block before the tipoff. When Kobe pulled up, the The announcement "He's here!" was made over the microphone as Kobe pulled up. Yeaaaaahhhhh and Kobe, Kobe, Kobe chants could be heard throughout the park from the spectators.

Then I noticed him approaching tall and surrounded by secret service as he was pointing and instructing them "straight to the court." Let's put on a show, he said as he headed right up to the bench after passing through the gate that leads to the court. I instinctively accepted what was going to happen at that time.

The absurd aspect was that Greg Jones and Moochie Norris, two of my closest buddies, were the stars of the DC squad we were playing against in New York. Two of DC's Finest were G Jones and Moochie (as I like to call them). Both had successful professional careers and played

9

at a high level in college. In the USBL, the three of us played together and set numerous records. Together, we were dangerous. But on this particular day, we were at cross purposes. But why did we have to play my hometown team on Kobe's visitation day? Once the ball was in the air, it made no difference; it was us vs them.

Kobe inbounded the ball to me, and as I started to dribble it up the floor, the fans started cheering loudly in anticipation. Let me see that, Kobe said as he walked over to me. I dropped the ball after my final dribble at that time, and he took over at that point. Let's go, I exclaimed as I raised my hands in the air. I'm well-known to and frequently seen by The Park. If they get to see Kobe Bryant live, this will likely be the first and final time, so he should be the feature.

I always do my job and let the guess players shine. I've played at the Park with Derrick Anderson, Byron Davis, Jamal Crawford, and Vince Carter, but I just knew this game would be the best.

Both teams had their share of highlights in the game, but we stole the show. Outside, it even started to rain. The games typically go inside the Gauchos gym in the Bronx when it rains. Kobe refused to go inside, so we remained outside. The Mamba desired to remain outside and have fun in the downpour. Having fallen in love with the ambience, he wanted to soak it all up. Be cautious and just keep moving forward, he added as he walked over to me. Quit jumping he said. At that point, a man worth $70 million was on the playground playing on concrete in the pouring rain. He was a real one. I grew more enamored.

That game and its highlights have amassed millions of views and become popular online. Being a part of that makes me grateful, and I appreciate the feedback. People frequently inquire about what it was like to play alongside Kobe. While I may provide examples and share this tale, words cannot adequately capture the experience.

After our epic basketball game at Rucker Park, I had the good fortune to sit down with Kobe. One of my favorite basketball memories involves taking the court with Kobe during that incredible game. After the game, we headed to Mr. Chows, which was at the time one of his faves. I had the chance to get to know both Kobe the athlete and Kobe Bryant the person. His extensive knowledge of a variety of topics, from business to sports, piqued my interest.

We had a unique bond in our love of the game. He became so engrossed in the game that he began sketching designs of it on napkins while describing to me his strategy and how he would play, step, and move beyond the defense. As soon as he would score, he would start planning his next opportunity to make a play. I discussed with him my ideas on how I could trick the defense with only a move or the way I dribbled. I had a belief that the example of a puppet master could back up my belief and carry out the pictures that I have verbally drawn. We had a lot of common interests since we were zealots

Even before Mamba Mentality became a thing, our minds were so similar that our thoughts and approaches to the game were parallel. He used his words to create images in my head, and I genuinely thought I was speaking to myself. Given that it was Kobe, I never discussed that with anyone. Kobe's level made it impossible for anyone to comprehend that our mentalities couldn't be parallel. They didn't realize it, though.

I was astounded that Kobe paid attention to my views and valued my contribution to the discourse. It made sense because I practiced what I preached and practiced it repetitively. One of the reasons I appreciate Kobe's game so much is that he approaches it the same way I did, using both his head and his feet. Footwork is something we emphasize a lot. Although I did work out my way, I wasn't as dedicated to my workouts as he was. This guy was crazy.

With peers, I would watch his games and predict what he would do next. from his choice of shots to his dribbling maneuvers. I was seriously engulfed. I was attentive.

I wish I had had the chance to meet him in college. Despite the fact that I am older than him, he helped me understand the game and opened up my thinking. He attested to the effectiveness of my

atypical approach to problem-solving. He could understand it because I did it my way, it was effective, and he saw me do it. At the time, I wasn't coaching, but I was my own instructor. Our discussions brought to a close my playing career in basketball. It supported me and helped me understand what I'm sharing today. I advanced.

My efforts to spread the "Mamba Mentality" to players and families around the world have been influenced, inspired, and driven by it. Kobe was a unique individual. Along with his brilliance, his aura and charisma made you pay attention to what he had to say. I was eager to watch him raise GiGi because he was such a wonderful father.

That was going to be the first player he would use to test his understanding from beginning to end.

I'll keep sharing and instructing with the same intention and attention. With the exception that I'll approach it the Cheat Code way. Blessings and prayers are sent to Vanessa Bryant and everyone else who has lost a loved one.

We are all members of one large family in the world of basketball, and we support one another. We carry on the legacies of those who came before us, and I'll definitely carry on GiGi and Kobe's.

God bless you everyone!

To all the wonderful people that we, (our basketball family), have recently lost in

Kobe Bryant

Gianna Bryant

Jamar "Silent" Board

Tyron "Alimoe" Evans

Troy "Escalade" Jackson

Flash

Pat Summit

Ed Sheffy

Big Jeff

Simmeon Williams

Eric "Hands"

Holly wood

Coach John Thompson Jr.

Vincent "Murph" Murphy

David Edwards

Hank Gathers

Jamal Jackson

Charles Harrison

Corey "Bink" Royster

Reggie Lewis

David Ed- wards

Lee Green

John Strickland

David Ed- wards

Lee Green

Hank Gathers

Jamal Jackson

Charles Harrison

PREFACE

OUR BELIEFS ARE so scattered, that we have no resilience. We can not effectively immunize ourselves to the opinions of others. In sports, one of the greatest adversities is public opinion. Who's good, who's better, who's not that good, they could be great, and we listen to those opinions and other rationals about ourselves. Regardless if it's the truth or not, we listen and it affects us. We allow opinions to occupy space in our minds, and it sits at the table of thought in our brains. When decisions are being made, those thoughts come to the front to challenge you. There is a mental battle that goes on before you go onto a field, court, gym and even before you touch a ball. That's the very first battle that has to be won before you can compete in anything. That battle never stops and you have to stay in control of it. What you allow, is a part of what you will become. Whether it's good for you or not, you allow it in your space, you consume it, you will become it. It's important to remember the old quote, "you are what you eat." It's all about your intake.

It's been said that playing sports is 90% mental. Coaches have to game plan and scout to help athletes prepare. Players have to train, learn concepts, focus and play through situations displaying mental toughness to overcome the physical and mental demands. These things take a great toll on athletes and and will determine an athletes success. It also seems true that both coaches and players have to "think the game." Being a Coach, I can confirm that it's true, we all have to do what's necessary to put our players in the best position possible to succeed and it all starts before you step on the playing field. A healthy and positive thought process is required for players and coaches to be successful on all levels. To be able to think the game, you have to be a student of the game and learn as much as you can. That way your thoughts will have answers. The key is to search for answers for every scenario. There are so many answers and a lot to figure out. Listen to wisdom and wisdom will guide you through the tough times. Learn form veterans, they've been through it and can give you a blueprint of what's ahead of you.

To maximize your talents, abilities, and take control of your thought process, you first have to realize that all these things are controlled by you! Not your parents, not your coaches, or trainers, all though they will try, and some not inadvertently, it's just the nature of the beast. People involved in any aspect of your development, want to be a part of the reason you're successful, and believe they know what's best for you. They will have to realize that only you can determine an outcome. Nobody can play the game for you. As long as I have been coaching, I have never seen a kid make a shot when someone yells at them to "Shoot it," when they're not ready or focusing on taking that shot. Maybe some have thrown up a shot and a have a little luck and it goes in. The majority of the time, if you're not focusing or concentrating on taking a shot, you won't make it. The key is what you think!

Sports discussions, biggest debates always boil down to comparisons. This player is a better shooter, or he is a better passer. Comparison's are healthy and necessary.It's true that no two players are alike. Everyone is different. But what really makes a player better than another player? Each individual brings something to the table that no one else has. You are unique. When everyone can do the same things, what separates you? Everyone has a special gift. That gift that they possess, is to be shared. You can cause a positive feeling or reaction to people with your uniqueness. It's something that's special and dear to you, so you want it to be your best. This is your stage of discovery. Your discovery period is all about finding out who you are as a player. The things you do well and the things that are comfortable and come natural to you.

When playing sports, you prepare for these moments to share the things that you are really good at. The excitement, the passion and appreciation is all because of how you perform. The response from others, feed you the energy and support that you desire. Your game is what's going to separate you from the rest and bring that excitement and motivation you need to give more of yourself. You are what the coaches, parents and spectators feed off of. You are the focus.

Look at it this way; Your game is entertainment. There are people who want to see you do good. Parents want to brag, your friends want to let everyone know they're your friends, coaches want to showcase you, evaluators want to write about you, all because people want to be attached to what they feel is good or successful. But a part of our development is "Focus." Amidst all of this, we have to focus on the process. The process are the experiences created on the journey to the reward. If you ask retired players, what was the greatest part about their career, most will answer the competition (playing the game) and the next answer will be the journey. To some, the journey is a greater experience than the reward. Trying to figure out your style and your game, is a part of the process. The feedback from those around you and your peers is a part of the process. The feedback you get that has an effect on you, is a part of the process. Whether you agree with the feedback or not, you will still have to deal with it mentally. Take it for what it's worth.

We spend time worrying what others think, and want to impress everyone, but all you have to do is impress you! You will affect your family, friends and your audience regardless of how you do it, just do it your way. Your way is always the right way in the end. You have to make the commitments and sacrifices to make it work. The process has many stages in development. First you decide that playing is what you want to do. Your mind has to be made up that it's what you want. You have to develop mental toughness, because so many things will try and take you off your path. You have to love what you do and have fun doing it. Be a student of the game. Study the game and find out the details. Be like a sponge and absorb all that you can. Watch it, listen to it and figure out the nuances and the purpose of why players do what they do when it relates to developing and winning. One of the key things of becoming a great player is to learn and master the basics and fundamentals.

Basketball is a very simple game, but has complicated situations within the game. The simplicity are the fundamentals. What's complicated is learning it all and applying it to the situations. Making it translate. Taking what you are learning and applying it successfully to the game. I can't stress enough that pickup basketball is the best way to develop as a player. Kids need to play the game freely and discover who they are as players. That's the biggest key to development, "Discovery."

Let them play and teach them the way. Guide them and give them feedback as they play the game their way. Allow them to have fun and push them to play hard while having fun. Let them enjoy the game and fall in love with it. Self evaluations are also important. Evaluate yourself and learn more about yourself by doing so. You will always be your toughest critic. Nobody has the right to be more critical of your game as you are of yourself. It's not being hard on yourself. It's just not settling for mediocrity or having lower standards than what you want for yourself. If you can't be that, ask a Coach, ask a friend, but start somewhere with the evaluation process.

A TRUE evaluation and not the evaluations that reads, "can get to the hole off the bounce, hard worker and can create shots for others." That's not a true evaluation. True evaluations are your basketball blueprint. It details everything from strengths and weaknesses. It gives the interested reader an idea of who you are as a player. It's constructive criticism of your game in its rawest form, stripped and uncut and ready to build up the player in you. Someone should be able to read your evaluations and almost know your game before they see you play. You don't buy a house just because the ad says, great bath and shower, modern kitchen and large master suite. You need more information, floor plans and the details. Your environment is also key. That includes character, work ethic, smart working, attitude, preparation, commitment, focus and fun. This is what's going to wrap up all of your developmental process into who you are as a player. Last but not least, knowing who you are as a player as mentioned before is the start, but it's also the ending. Who you are and who you will become as a player, is knowing what you will bring to the table and having confidence to do it.

The process of development has a lot of challenges and a lot of steps. So how do you become a great player? There are no easy ways, particular blueprints, or one right way to do it. Greatness comes from within. You have to do your part. have an imagination and goals ahead of you. You can't know how, If you don't study the game and other great players. You need your goals to drive you. You need a discovery period to find you. You need imagination to make you and you need the confidence to do you! A story of imagination and goal chasing, that is probably the biggest carbon copy we've seen in sports, is Kobe Bryant compared to Michael Jordan. Everybody wanted to be Mike growing up. Walk like him, play like him, wag your tongue like him. But Kobe did it the best. The thing that made Kobe great, was that Kobe took parts of his game from Michael Jordan and made them his own.

Kobe played his own style and his own way. He mastered the basics and fundamentals. He learned from Mike and he added what he had learned to his game. That helped him earn 5 NBA Championships as well as becoming a first ballot Hall of Fame player, and one of the NBA All Time greats. Hate it or love it, he created success from what he's learned from others and made it his own. Most great players have all modeled their games after other players, but the thing that you possess that's different from the others, is the ingredient that makes it your own. For Kobe, it was his mentality known as the "Mamba Mentality." To sum it up, it's being the best version of yourself. Separate yourself from the comparisons. Be the best you, that you can be. The mental game is a very important part of anything that you do when seeking success.

YOU DOUBT YOURSELF more when you lack confidence, Which brings me to another question; what are the best ways to maximize confidence? Lack of confidence will have you doubting your capabilities. It's important to believe in what you can do. Confidence levels come from your beliefs. The more you believe, the more you can achieve. We focus a lot on our weaknesses, instead of also concentrating on our strengths. Remember your mental thoughts are everything. What you focus on the most, will take the lead in you're game. Confidence will help you get to your goals faster. Always put more time into your strengths than weaknesses. Your strengths will help your confidence rise and mentally heal your lack of confidence in your weaknesses. Your thoughts will go from, I can't go left to, you can't stop me regardless of my left. Someone will tell you different, but trust me from experience. Strengthening your strengths will help build your confidence.

As a coach, my teams have beaten a lot of good teams and we had less talent. One reason for that was because we attacked their weaknesses while maximizing our strengths. I didn't have the best players coming up, but my teams always competed on a high level and I got the best out of every player regardless of skill set because of their confidence. My kids played like the best, even when they were not. Yes, we also work on our weaknesses to become complete players, but strengthening your strengths, I will repeat, makes the confidence grow faster. That's half the battle. I have been searching for answers for myself for a long time, and it's so much to learn and more to find out. A lot of players have been searching for their confidence for a long time and also trying to figure out who they are as players. I have some answers and will help you solve some of your problems, and things that I have found in my journey's, I will share them with you. A lot of questions will be answered and gems will be shared in this book. It's called "Cheat

Code," because as a player, I was different from my peers. I was ahead of my time. I could play with anybody and play any position or any role and be successful. I understood the game and the why's. I have an answer and an adjustment for almost everything. I will unveil the things that I have used to successfully develop myself, as well as develop other young and inexperienced players. I will share stories and a few simple mental concepts, that when applied will help any level player, regardless of skill set, and maximize the player they are to be. My intent is for players to restore their confidence, learn how to translate everything they learn in the game and be their best self! Coaches and Parents, will also learn how to understand and be a part of player development. Development is a lot of things, getting bigger, stronger, faster, or becoming a better ball handler or shooter. But we are focusing on becoming a CONFIDENT PLAYER, becoming a smarter player and being the best YOU that YOU can be.

"I found out that their weren't too many limitations, if I did it my way"

- Lonnie "L-Train" Harrell aka "Prime Objective"

CHAPTER I:
MY WAY

I BELIEVE IN all things the very first step of any process is a thought. We think about what to do, how to do it, then figure out a solution to get it done. There are so many questions to be answered in the process, but the first fundamental question should be; What do I want to accomplish? The answer to that should be your goals. Those things are the reason why you're doing whatever it is that you choose to do. Everything has an end goal. In between the start and that end goal, is the Process. The process are the things that happen to you during the steps taken to get to that end goal. It's your journey. How are you going to make it there? What are the things you have to do, to get there? We always get advised by people that tell us to, stay focused, lock in and concentrate on what we are trying to accomplish.. But how do you focus with all the distractions, instigators, handlers, coaches, evaluators, trainers and parents, pulling, tugging, teaching, telling you to do it this way or that way? How can you stay focused? How can you develop? How can you find success with so many distractions during the process to reach your ending?

The answers you will find on your journey, will be what drives you. Your journey will make you. You will find that the things you need to build your confidence and develop into the player that you want to be, are right under your nose. You were born with those tools. No one can give them to you. They are a part of you. Your journey will help you discover them. This goes for players, coaches, parents, trainers and all that's involved in the development of young athletes. It's a simple concept, but it really starts with learning who you are and learning the game. Learning the game consist of, the basics, fundamentals, evaluations, studying players, styles of play, acknowledging strengths, recognizing weaknesses and a lot of other things. Each player needs to be aware of these things to maximize their potential and peak their development. But we can not skip the process.

In my era, we all learned how to play the same way. We all have the same story that we tell our way. The difference is our process. There will always be bumps and adversity during your process. But those bumps in the road are a part of your journey. When you go on a road trip, knowingly that it's going to be a long ride, you pre- pare for that trip. You fill up the gas tank, you check the oil, you put air in your tires and you make sure the weather is going to be fair for this long journey. Let's even say you're driving the best car on the market. Let's say a Bentley. This Bentley is you. You're the best of the best on this journey, but on this journey, you are on a road and the next exit is 20 miles and your gas is low, the weather is bad, it's a storm and you can barely see through your windshield. It's dark outside and you feel like you're the only one on this road but you know you're not. Its cars ahead of you and behind you. You're wondering why the cars are driving so fast passing you but you're in a nice car. It's a lot of reasons why this road and this journey is different for you than the other cars on the road. It's the same roads being traveled, but each of you deal with the journey differently. You know your situation, your gas level, how much you can see, how you deal with storms. Your journey and experience is different. But you all are going in the same direction.

That car that passed you, could have traveled that road many of times. It could have just got on the road, it could be a million things. Then you finally make it to that rest stop and you see the cars that passed you on the road. You caught up. You were worried at first because you felt you were being left behind on that road and the cars were passing you during your struggles, but it's how you had to deal with your journey. It's how you processed your situation and you felt you had to take your time to get there. But once you made it, all the cars that passed you on the way, were there to. No matter what happens on that road, you can get a flat tire, car can break down, you might need a tow truck etc. That is a part of your journey. Your team, coaches, games you play, you're go- ing to have things on your road that's going to slow you down or try and hold you back from reaching your goals. That's a part of the process. You can't skip it. You can't throw the whole car away while you're on your journey. You can't just pull over and call carmaker and get a new car and then continue. You have to make it to your destination while you're on this trip. The way you arrive to the place that's destined for you, is your unique way of perseverance. We can't speed up because everyone else is speeding. We drive different, we have to drive at the speed we are comfortable with and keep pushing ourselves knowing that we will make it there. We rather make it there late, than never make it at all.

WHEN I STARTED to play basketball, I played at my playground in Southeast D.C. with my friends at Malcolm X Elementary School. My Neighborhood is called Congress Park. Back in the 80's, there were so many distractions. DC was known as the murder capital of the U.S., the crack epidemic was going on, poverty was at an all time high, and you had to fight to live. Fighting was your test of strength everyday. Whether you were fighting with your friends, or fighting someone from another neighborhood at elementary or middle school, it was a fight everyday. But it was only two ways to live your life as a kid back then. Best described by the artist Christopher "Biggie Smalls" Wallace, "Either you're slinging crack rock, or you got a wicked jump shot."

As a young kid, growing up on the playgrounds in the 80's, it was one of the greatest era's in College and Professional basketball history. I watched a lot of football and basketball during this time and I would record the games to watch on my own TV and VHS player that I had got for Christmas one year. I was a big fan of the players, didn't really like teams. I watched David Rivers, Danny Manning, Sean Elliott, Michael Jordan, Pearl Washington, Len Bias, Pat Ewing, Baskerville Holmes and David Wingate (the men). I also watched Cheryl Miller, Dawn Staley, Sheryl Swoopes, Tina Thompson and Cynthia Cooper (the women). One of my best teachers was the time I spent alone watching other players play and playing by myself. Playing alone allowed me to experiment with ideas and imagine things without others opinions. One place where I spent time experiment- ing other than outside on the courts, was at home in my room. I played on baskets that I made from hangers and cardboard. The balls were made of paper wrapped with tape or even rolled up socks. When outside on the play- ground, I used the monkey bars as baskets, baskets made from bicycle rims nailed on trees, Milk crates nailed too walls, or, on the real basketball courts at the school yard when the older guys wasn't playing late at night. Whether I was playing basketball or football, I would play multiple positions and imagine that I was playing a full game.

In those times, I could experiment and copy the things I've seen others do. I copied my friends, the older guys I'd watch play, or the players on TV. There wasn't any- body there to tell me how to do it right, or if I'm doing it wrong. I would continue to do the moves I'd seen other players do, and then get so used to doing them, that I would start making those moves mine. I would take what I saw and add my style, and it would become a part of me. There was no right or wrong way to do it if I made it mine. During that time, the only games that came on during the weekends were the Sixers, Lakers, Celtics or Pistons. Being from DC, the Washington Bullets came on Tuesday's. I never watched games on Tuesdays, so I didn't know anything about the Bullets. My favorite pros were Moses Malone, Bobby Jones, Moe Cheeks and Dr. J for the Sixers. Magic, Kareem, Michael Cooper and Worthy for the Lakers. Dennis Johnson, Robert Parrish,

Larry Bird, Kevin McHale and Reggie Lewis for the Celtics and Isaiah Thomas, Joe Dumars, Dennis Rodman and Vinny Johnson for the Pistons. After seeing them play on the weekends, what ever game came on, I would copy what I saw the whole week until the weekend came around again, to watch the next games.

During this time, my best friend Paul and I use to hang together everyday. When we weren't watching wrestling on Saturday Mornings, we were outside playing a sport. We would play one on one football games. Simulate the kickoff, being the Quarterback, running back and receiver, or we would be playing full court on a court we made outside with bike rims and crates. The courts could be anywhere and on anything. Sometimes they were even across the street from each other. We just loved to play. But most of the time I played basketball, I was alone. Only my mom knew that because it drove her crazy! Either in the house running into walls making noise, or staying out past my curfew and she having to scream out the window, Lonnnniiiiiieeeeeeee, or send my sister and cousin up to the court to get me. They would be mad because they had to stop whatever they were doing or watching on TV to come and get me.

One of my favorite games I played alone, on my bedroom baskets, was a full court game I created. I had a hanger made basket on the top henges of the door, and the other court was above the window on the opposite end and was made of cardboard. I destroyed my mother's paint because I used the strongest tape so the courts wouldn't fall. There was enough room for me to move in a straight line maybe 8 steps. My bed took up most of the room.

The vibe for me, was playing in the Los Angeles Forum. The game was right hand versus left hand. I would shoot at one basket with my left and the other with my right. Some games it would be the Sixers versus the Lakers and I would be the starting 5 from each team. "Magic comes down, goes behind the back and lobs it too Worthy for two. Or Moe Cheeks with the steal, kicks it to Bobby Jones for 3!" I would imagine the entire game. Another game I would play alone, was Magic versus Bird, one on one full court. I would shoot with my left hand for Bird, because I saw him use his left with ease. This game I would also mimic both of their styles as de- tailed as shooting like bird from behind the ear, and skipping down court like Magic backing my man in position to shoot the running hook. I could really play like these guys because I copied them so much. My solo games and my imagination, was developing me as a player. I had no clue that's what i was doing. I would do this everyday, not knowing that I was developing my left hand (off hand, I'm a righty). I was developing my left hand touch and comfortability. Playing alone using both hands was the only way I knew how to make it a competitive game and distinguish between my imaginative players. Imagination is everything!

After copying so much, I began to get creative with my moves and my shots. My favorite shot was a fadeaway where I would jump sideways and dive on my bed as I released the paper ball. My friends had the same bas- kets at their homes and we would play against each other. We had a league and a game schedule. We would go to each other homes, lock ourselves in the room and play one on one until our moms couldn't take the noise, or the BOOM, from the holes we would put in the walls from hard fouls, being pushed into the wall, and just be- ing physical boys. The games were really intense. I would do my fadeaway on to their bed, and they couldn't believe how I could make that shot with so much accuracy. I had done it so many times, that in my mind, I just figured if I do it, I'm going to make it and I did. That was my introduction to mental development. Even my in- door trick shots would work when I played outside on real baskets with my friends. Today, I still walk in gyms and call shots with friends and my players. I would walk in the gym and take my first shot from out of bounds, behind the backboard, or from half court underhanded, anything difficult or just a crazy shot. Making shots from crazy angles, left or right handed. Or just a deep shot, and I guess you figured, I would make it. I knew that I would make the shot before I would shoot it. Confidence is believing in what you know and not afraid to carry it out without any doubts while being prepared to carry out the task. Muscle memory goes for the brain as well. It's called "Mind over matter." I've taken so many shots over and over and in all situations, that I know how to make the shot.

Earlier in this chapter, I mentioned how I copied players and made their moves my own. I watched players today, copy James Harden's step back and do the move exactly how he does it. Kids come in the gym where I workout, doing the move and traveling and will say as a disclaimer, "that's not a travel, Harden does that." And I would return with, "Harden is in the NBA", and the NBA allows Harden to do his signature move. It's his move. Even NBA players copy the move. You have to earn the right to do what those guys are doing on that level. But what's allowed is you being you. You are unique.

Before all of the moves and being unique, you have to master the basics and fundamentals! You can't skip that part of the process. If you do, it will catch up with you later on in your career. The basics and fundamentals are the seed and soil of basketball. You can't grow without them. The greatest players of all time are masters of the fundamentals. Michael Jordan, Scottie Pippen and Kobe Bryant are at the top of the list. They are not the flashiest guys, they don't waste movement. Magic Johnson use fundamentals to throw his passes. Larry Bird used the basics to out smart his opponents. Dennis Rodman used them to box out and rebound. Those players mastered the fundamentals. Basics and fundamentals are a beauty in itself. I will never forget when I got to College at Georgetown University, Coach John Thompson Jr. told me that my game was pretty just playing hard. That I didn't need to try and be flashy. The game is pretty just the way you play it. The fundamental game itself is beautiful.

Once you master those things, then you can begin to be creative. I would have taken any players move and made it my own. Credit to the player, for the move, but I would have created my own version that worked for my game and my style. Steve Smith at the University of

Michigan State (one of my favorite college players), had this hesitation move he used to free himself enough space to make a play. He would do a fake spin with a hesitation, and then come back the same way after a hard plant. He would get the defenders feet flat and stuck and allow him to go pass them with ease. I would go on the court alone, practice the move, and then try it out on my friends and understand exactly how and why it works. Once I understood those things, I would take it further and add a setup to it, so the defender could never see it coming. I used to do it so much that older players saw it coming and would wait on it. So I had to add a setup so they wouldn't see it coming and it made the move unstoppable. It's safe to say, that my "Smitty", was better than Steve's. If we were playing a team and the player that I was guarding scored on me and made a nice move and got the crowd going wild, I would come down and do my Smitty. It would freeze the whole defense and I would drive and get an easy dunk. I would make sure that I made it look easy and take the life out of whatever my opponent had just done. It made the game more fun for me.

I have taken this approach in everything that I do when it comes to developing players. When I played football, Eric Dickerson was my favorite player. Although I was a good Quarterback, I wanted to be like Eric Dickerson. I copied how he ran, how he moved and I even copied his style. I had all the equipment he wore, the goggles, eye- glass cage, neck roll, #29, tape over my cleats and drew the Adidas sign on them down to every detail. I did this while playing Quarterback, Flanker and Safety. And I looked good copying him. I pulled it off. I was tall, so copying his stride and movements, made me glide through the line and taught me to run using my length.

But I didn't know all that, I just saw what I liked and copied it. I wanted to be like my favorite players. Similar to Kobe copying Mike. Professional athletes know what they're doing and why they're doing it. Younger players don't. But if you can master it and understand why, it can make you great.

Everybody wanted to be like Michael Jordan growing up, Kobe Bryant actually did it. And now he's a first bal- lot Hall of fame inductee, adding 5 Championship rings to his mantle. Kobe studied Mike and made a Kobe ver- sion. It's nothing wrong with copying something someone great does and making it your own. But don't skip the basics and fundamentals. Mike, Kobe and Scottie Pippen were the greatest fundamentally sound players to play the game. They mastered the fundamentals and added their flare to it.

The game conditions us to get it right. Trainers coaches and others train you to get it right their way. But your best bet is to get it right your way. You have to retrain yourself so that you can discover all that you can do. People will always have expectations of you, but your expectations matter most. You have to figure it out!

I always played the game my way. I listened to my coaches, I did what they wanted me to do, but some thought I was trying to be fancy when I did certain things, but I wasn't. I was playing basketball my way and how I learned. Magic Johnson and Larry Bird were my two favorite players during their run in the 80's. I copied them so much and could do everything they did. I would go on the court and say I'm Magic one game and i'm Larry Bird the next game. And I would play just like them and do moves that I saw them do, down to the timing. When I got on a team for the first time, the Coach put me at Center because I was the tallest. I wanted to handle the ball and you know the typical Centers back then, didn't handle the ball. But i didn't worry. I watched Magic and Bird who were respectively 6'9 and 6'10. I watched them both rebound and start the break, that's one way to handle the ball and I watched Bird shoot corner 3's and turn around jump shots and post up. So I could do those things from copying those players. I know a lot of Coaches tell kids not to do this or not to do that, and most of the times, it's because the kids aren't efficient and consistent in doing them. But I could and i was confident doing them. So I was successful at playing Center my way. When I got to High School, I was in the paint again because I was one of the taller players. No problem, I played my game at Center and was successful and got a full scholarship to Georgetown to be a guard. See how that works? Let me explain it.

We have all experienced either ourselves or our kids be- ing the tallest and getting "stuck" down in the paint be- cause of it. But we want our kids to develop into ball handlers and shooters. Youth teams are not responsible for individual player development. Some do it because that's what they do, but most teams are trying to develop a winning team. Being tall is an asset because you can't teach height. But, if you don't have the skills to play out on the wings in game situations and not efficient and consistent, that's not the time to be trying too.

A position is just a word and a formality that will get you on the floor. The only position that I know is "Basketball Player." I knew who I was as a player by the age of 14. That's when I started to play organized ball. I came in the game ready. I knew my game, i was confident and I played it my way. But the key is, you have to be ready for what you want. If you going places expecting some- thing to happen or change you into the player you want to be, then you have it all wrong. To play your way, you have to put in the work to be able to say you have a way, and it has to be efficient, confident and translate. behind it. I grew and grew as a player because I never stopped adding to my game. I was excited to show something new I could do. When I learned new tricks, I couldn't wait to get to practice and try them. I watched Dennis Rodman rebound and copied him and would go and grab 20 rebounds because I saw him tip the ball to open spots where he only knew he would tip it and hustle to go get it. It worked for me. I had to prove myself to coaches, and I didn't mind that. That was my way, what's yours?

"Believe in individuality and the freedom to be whoever you want to be." -Donatella Versace

"We do what we are trained to do, we do what we were bred to do, we do what we were born to do" - Leonidas (300 Movie)

Chapter II:
FIGURE IT OUT

ONE REASON I was successful at playing basketball was being a great listener. I listened to my coaches, to players and the older guys that played outside on the week- days after they got off work in my neighborhood. Early in the mornings on the weekends when players from other neighborhoods were allowed to come to the courts and play, Malcolm X basketball courts were the place to be Saturday and Sunday at 8 o'clock am. Although it was in a rough neighborhood, the street guys respected the courts and the players. Some of them could play and would never miss a game.

I listened to how the older guys would talk on the court and mostly how competitive they were and their words. I listened to them after the games when they would sit around and drink beers and gatorade, while giving their own recaps to the games they just played. So much dialogue being taken in, I felt a part of the game before they even allowed me to play with them. It was like listening to live evaluations. The losing team players would go back and forth about what and who lost the game, how they lost it and pointing fingers. I learned accountability from that. Every man has to do his part for a team to be successful. But remember, you can't criticize if you can't be criticized and honor your part and be accountable. The winning team would say good things about their team- mates and give their version of and playbacks of shots, moves or plays that they remembered and how it made them feel when it happened. That made me feel good and I wasn't playing. But I remembered that feeling when I would play. I loved to be celebrated. I wanted my team- mates to say good things about me. So when i played, I played to impress them.

Later on that helped me become a great teammate, because I wanted that feeling for myself and others.

When I first started out, I always got a new basketball for my birthday or Christmas. As soon as I put my hands on it, I would take it everywhere with me. If I went to the ice cream truck, I had my ball. When I had to walk 12 blocks to the store and back, I would put all the groceries in one hand and dribble my ball there and back. I would take it everywhere I could. Once my errands where complete, I would run out the door to the basketball court. I would shoot and play until the older guys would come and take over the court after they got off work. That's when they would take my ball and have me sit on the sidelines until they were done with MY new ball. I really didn't mind, because I really loved watching them play. I was eager to get out there and show them how good I felt I was. I had already thought I was better than they were in my mind, I was waiting for the chance to play with them so I could show them.

I would have thoughts about how they played and felt this guy should have taken another dribble and drifted on that shot, or he should have made that a bounce pass, or that shot should have been off the glass. I was detailed in my observations and a sponge at the same time, as a 12 year old. If I saw something I liked, I was trying that as soon as it was my turn to take the court. I understood skill sets early. I was doing things and practicing the way I'd seen others play, and copying the pros I watched on TV. I knew these guys weren't doing what I was do- ing, because these guys had jobs and families. I thought about it, watched it and played it all day. I fell in love with basketball, I spent all of my time playing on my hoops in the house, and on the court all day and night when nobody else was playing. I stayed on the court un- til it was time for me to go home for dinner. Even then my Moms would have to send someone up to the court to get me. I loved playing. I was ready to play with the older men.

I played basketball because I loved it, and I wanted to play it. I was free as a bird. Being free and able to play how you want to play can be a gift and a curse without the right guidance. The gift being the freedom to play and figure it out. The curse is, some don't figure it out or have the proper guidance to help them figure it out. I was fortunate enough to figure it out with help from the older guys who saw the potential in me and always gave me tips. I had the proper guidance and I made the game my own. To play free, you have to have an imagination and learn the basics and fundamentals of the game. Developing an IQ along the way is a must. You have to be a student of the game and pay attention to the lessons and the details. Once I learned the fundamentals, all the studying of other players raised my IQ, I learned how to play the game and I was able to manipulate the game and opponents. I learned to be deceptive, I learned to make my defenders puppets. I studied everybody and everything. I watched how the coaches would interact with certain players and how the players responded. I paid attention to how the fans would act and respond to what happens in the game. I watched everything! I knew what every player on the floors strengths and weaknesses were.I even interacted with the opposing coach to test his mentality. Oh yeah, coaches don't get a pass either, they have to be tested as well. Everybody is not built for the moment. Situations and moments are what separate the good from the great. You have to have mental toughness to compete and stay focused in key situations and moments. Mental toughness holds every- one accountable.

Most coaches don't have time or take the time out to develop players. When a coach says, "we develop players," more than likely, the development has a ceiling. Coaches have to Coach and develop their team. During the sea- son, coaches concentration is on their system and philosophy. So individual player development is limited. It's what you add to help the teams needs that will give you an opportunity. The typical Grassroots coach does not develop individual players, because they're trying to win. That usually consists of getting the best players to build the best team. They develop teams by building them like the free agent process of the NBA with no salary cap. It's important to do the work yourself. Hav- ing the fundamentals and knowing what you bring to the table gives you an advantage when joining a team. The expectations are what you are capable of doing. Not what you want to do, or want to learn to do. It's a lot of timing involved in the development process. That will make you or break you. It could be the right place at the right time, or the right play at the wrong time. That de- pends on you.

My team practice experience as a player was different from other players. I didn't just go to practice to learn the plays and run sprints. I wanted to learn why the plays worked, the options, and how the defense would try and stop it. My focus was always to pay attention to the options and the defenses reactions. I knew what I could do, so I needed to know my spots, and how the defense responded to what I was doing. Whenever the coach gave me advice, I accepted it, but I also kept my head free because I saw something different. I saw more in the game. This might sound as if I was doing my own thing, or showing up the coach, NEVER. I ran the plays. But if a play broke down, or the defense stopped a part of the play, I had a counter. I would be able to make a play. That helped me out late in games as well.

It's normal to experience things differently. We have different characteristics, morals and values that allows us to think for ourselves from our previous experiences. So we all have a different approach. I liked to hear about other players and coaches philosophy's, I could learn something to add to mine. Anything that would make me better. If we were football players and I run a 4.5 40 yard dash and you run a 4.2, our routes will not get the same results and attention because of your speed versus mine and our differences in style how we run the routes . Defenses will play players differently because of skill sets. You don't close out on a shooter, the same way you would close out on a driver.

You're not going to defend Kyrie Irvin the same way you

defend Rajon Rondo. They're two players with two totally different skill sets and styles of play. They both experience the same game different way. They will produce different results. Kyrie scoring 20 points and dishing out 12 assist will not have the same results in a game that Rondo posts identical numbers because of their playing styles and the different effects they have on the game. Don't compare yourself to another player. Experience the game your way and make it yours.

Experiences are also different for coaches and players. The key is to have the two intertwined, and make them work together. This is what makes you a more coachable player, leader and an extension of your coach on the floor. Being able to articulate those experiences with your coaches will put you in a favorable space with your coach. That's if you are doing the other things asked of you, like hustling, good defense, playing smart and competing. Coaches don't want to coach effort. That is expected and should be automatic if you truly love the game.

I didn't have a big workout routine, nor did I try to lift all the weights in the weight room. I jumped rope a lot and did calisthenics because that helped me stay in good physical condition. It enabled me to run the floor on both ends. I had stamina to play the whole game, and out run my opponent. People hated guarding me be- cause I never stopped running. I never got pushed around. But those things are definitely a part of it. I did what worked for me. Having lean muscle mass, the first thing players thought was that I was weak and could be pushed around. Neither was true. Because I developed my skill set, I could play at a faster pace without allow- ing defenders to keep up with me or slow me down. My skill set matched my athleticism.

I found creative ways to make the game mine! It took time for coaches to take to my style. I know that sounds crazy, for a coach to take to me, but when you're young and playing grassroots basketball, that's the time to figure out who you are as a player and what the game is all about. I remember hearing a former NBA player say, he would never let his son play on a team that the coach won't allow him to run around and play the game his way. He said that's why Steph Curry and Westbrook are so dangerous. He compared them to unleashed pit-bulls in a room of people. Which is more dangerous in that room, a pit-bull on the leash, or one without a leash?

That's why Steph Curry and Russell Westbrook are so dangerous, they can do anything they want on the court. They are really good players who have mastered their skills and know how to play the game. Their coaches trust that they will play the right way and give the team a chance to win. Young players don't need to be over coached early on, they need to be taught. Coaching is more of game managing, team development and teaching team concepts. Grass roots should be taught how to play the game on the fly and as you go. It's not a easy job because you want to win, but for the future of your players careers, you want to prepare them for future success. Coaches evaluate players to help them learn more about the players game and assess their skills. It's a long process of development and the early stages are key. Players need to be taught the fundamentals and how to figure things out on the court, while dis- covering who they are as players.

A lot of teams I played on, I started out on the bench, or got benched for making a play that was considered fancy or untimely. But there was always a method to the madness. I was ahead of the game at my time. There wasn't a lot of players my height that possessed the skills that I had. They didn't know what to do with me. That was on all levels that I have played on. But every time I got the opportunity, in practice or in games to show what I could do, I did me. Don't get this wrong, I wasn't selfish. I played team ball, but I would create opportunities to score for myself or anyone and make it look easy. As a kid, I was allowed to do that playing pickup games in the park. As I got to High School, I started learning structure, fundamentals, time and score and situational basketball. In College I started learning about systems, timing and execution. The Pro's was a whole other level of thought. If I could only have $100 for every time I was told, "It's not going to be easy, when you get to the next level." When I got to those lev- els, everyone looked at me play and thought it was easy. I was confident in what I could do and that's what I did. The only difference to me in competition was the players size and strength. I knew skill. I played against so many really good players and I played so much, every player I got in front of was similar to someone I had already played before in some kind of way. I played against so many great ball handlers, it wasn't many moves that I haven't seen. I could guess what a player was going to do, but a you could never stop a shot maker. Players that can put the ball in the basket many kinds of ways are deadly.

In 1996, I went un drafted and signed with the Orlando Magic. My first scrimmage with the Orlando Magic, I had an amazing and entertaining game. I hit threes, made nice passes and made plays. I rebounded, started the break, I was having a great game. Then to seal the deal, I will never forget, what happened on an inbound play. I was on defense, the offensive player, ran to the ball and slipped as the ball came in. I ran to get the steal and the player fell at my feet. I recovered the ball, and while doing so, I jumped over the falling defender and dribbled the ball behind my back and as I landed, I was close to the 3 point line, I stepped back and shot the 3 instead of going in for the layup. I made the shot, the crowd made a loud uproar and I was even featured on the local news after the game because of the plays I made. The next day at practice, I made an another amazing play against one of the veterans. I drove from the wing to an opening that I saw, it closed quickly by the forearm of the player who pretty me checked me in the ribs hard, but my footwork and handle was so good, when he checked me, I used his momentum and spun, as I was spinning, i drouth ball between my legs and came out the traffic and dunked it. I will never forget that play because Horace Grant, ran off the court screaming. He took me to lunch after practice and I was his road dog for about a month straight after that. Before I could en- joy that moment, one of the Coaches wanted to meet with me. We went into the empty locker room where the white board was, and he said to me... "You can't do everything, you have to pick one thing and be great at that." I didn't understand why at the time. I thought that the more I can do, the better. At that time, that wasn't how it worked. Playing on a team that had Penny Hardaway, who was a lottery pick and only a year or two ahead of me, the Coach was trying to tell me to define your role. Find one thing and do that great! When I finally figured that out, it was after my NBA opportunity. I had to step away with an injury, and then later with a failed physical for an enlarged heart. But what I realized was that your role will get you in. Once you're in, the Coach gets comfortable, you gain the trust, then you can open up your tool box when it's time or a need for an- other tool. It's always good to have all the tools, but be a specialist and master the use of one.

When I was with the Nets, another coach told me, "Fancy dribbling before you shoot is Street-ball." The shots were going in and I didn't understand what the issue was. It was perception. I was playing in the Summer in the EBC at Rucker Park when I got invited to work out for the New Jersey Nets. I had a reason for going between my legs or behind my back before I shot, it was a quicker way to get my shot off because the defense is expecting a move. But I did it to freeze them, just to get enough space to get my shot off. Anybody that tried to defend me would tell you that I had a fast twitch, erky jerky style. I was a good shooter, good ball handler and I could finish at the rim. Good defenders had to play me honestly. So they never knew when I was going to take a shot.

They knew I was going to shoot, but didn't know when. Coaches didn't want me to do that back then. Now look at the league today. Curry, Kyrie, Lillard, Harden... I was ahead of my time.

To all of the players out here working hard to become great athletes, don't overwork on drills in training that you don't do or use in the game, that's not going to develop YOUR GAME! A trainer or coach will not always recognize your game if you're doing the same drills over and over. Doing the same things over and over will make you a conditional robot. You want to be able to compete in any situation during a game.

You don't want a coach needing a specialist on the court, and you're going out the game because it's not your specialty. You want to be on the floor whenever your coach needs you. It's great to have all the tools, but sometimes all the tools aren't needed. But if a tool is needed, you'll have it handy and ready to work. Train your skills. Master footwork, basic ball handling and timing. Those things together makes a great ball handler. The best ball handlers react. You can predetermine rules unless you're that good.

How good are you really? What makes you different from other players? What will separate you from what everyone else is doing? I wasn't the best shooter, but I had more range than anybody and I could make difficult and hard shots. Having deep range, meant that I could get my shot off against defenses that sat back and wait- ed for me to attack them. It also meant that I would stretch the floor for my teammates. In High School I did it all. But when I received my scholarship to George-town, It was because I had a skill that could assist one of the most dominant bigs in college basketball, Alonzo Mourning. My job was to sit on the wing, make entry passes to him, and if he kicked it out, make the shot. It was hard to double team him because we had shooters everywhere. I could pass and shoot and that was my only role. I wasn't asked to do anything else. Being men- tally prepared, educated and knowing your game, will separate you. Playing like everyone else and being a conditional robot, you'll only win, lose or draw by favor. Expect everyone to work hard. The higher the level, the more they work. Find where you fit, master that, then be whatever a coach or team needs, when they need it. I made the decision to go to Georgetown. I could have went somewhere where a Coach could let me play my game. But during that time, I did not have the guidance or the information to recruit my coach for College. Yes I said "recruit my coach for College." So while I was at Georgetown, I filled my role and did the best I could in it.

"A lot of Coaches don't have an original thought in their brain."

- Mike Bozeman

Chapter III:
THE DEVELOPMENT PROCESS

THIS STAGE IS having an understanding of what the game is about. After uncorking your potential and getting a feel for the game, the process has begun. When the older guys finally saw me developing as I played with my friends, they then started choosing me to play with them. It didn't start out how I thought it would, because I didn't take into consideration how strong and how fast they played. I would try my moves and get the ball taken away. Throw weak passes and have the ball stolen. The next thing you know, I would be getting subbed out of a pickup game. Sitting on the side looking ridiculous, waiting for them to finish with my ball. They always used my ball and I had to stay as long as they were using it. I thought I was better than these guys. In my mind I was. In the physical form, I had to figure it out.

I had a lot of figuring out to do. I wondered how I could get over my struggles? It was time for trial and error. I had to take the things that I have learned to the court and take action. When I would play with the older guys, two of the quickest and most competitive guards, played together all the time. William "Fila" Brooks and John "Boo" Bivins. These were guys I looked up to because of how they dominated in sports. They were the best foot- ball players, baseball players, basketball players and would win most of the time they were out there. As soon

as I stepped on the court, they would always pressure me and make me turn the ball over. I couldn't get a shot off. All the things that I was learning and practicing had a different result when I played against quicker, faster and stronger players. One of the older guys told me,

"You can shoot. Just catch and shoot the ball." I wasn't shy at all. All you had to do is tell me that once. That was the day I began to show that I could play with them. My fit was discovered. I would run the floor hard. As soon as I got a pass, It was gone, the shot went up! I was hitting jumpers from all over the place. They trusted me and my role was to shoot the ball. That was my game at the time. This was a part of my development process that kept me on the court. This was all while I was in middle school.

Your roots and foundation is a part of your development.. If you come from a fundamental background, with fundamental teachers, you will more than likely be a fundamental player. If you come from a street ball background, then that's your foundation. Your soil is the brand of basketball you played growing up. That can be physical/soft, slow/fast paced etc. All those things are what makes up your game, it's. part of your process. Coaches go to certain regions for a certain style and type of players. The recruiting is to learn more and get to know the player. It gives the coaches an idea of the player that they're getting. It may be unfair to some, but players are sometimes judged by where they come from.

The experiences coaches have had with players from the same area before them, can influence a coaches decision. There are multiple other reasons, but this is one. This is why it's important to know who you are as a player and having your own identity to separate you is key. Perception goes a long way, but you get a chance to shake what people think by being consistent. Consistency is a part of being ready. If you are a shooter, you get one chance at a first impression. So being a consistent shooter, is more than chucking up shots. It's footwork, shooting the same way every time and knowing when to take shots. I had to learn these things over time, and this was one of the biggest lessons that I have learned from my older guys.

Finding out what type of player are you? What's unique about your game? And how do you figure that out is a part of your development process. A few common types are hustle players, smart players, great team players, scorers, shooters or defensive minded players. Those are typical categories. But i'm going to go deeper into the question and play on things we've talked about ear- lier. The key word in the question is "YOU." Remember, what's going to separate you? The few categories mentioned are typical to any player. But the best category is "you," and realizing what you bring to the table.

The best way to do this is to know your strengths. If it's shooting, shoot. But don't limit yourself to just spot up shooting. Learn how to shoot coming off of screens, off the dribble, fading, one leg, in transition, any way you can think of and master shooting. If you struggle with dribbling, don't spend all of your time trying to learn how. The key is to first master something, then gradually add as you go. If you're not great at anything, what's your use? Before you can say it, role players are specialist. The problem is everyone wants that one role, to be the man. Players are Bred and Born to be that. One of the biggest problems in the game is that most of the training is geared towards one on one basketball, when the game is played with 5 players on a team. Parents and players wonder why their workouts aren't translating. One reason is because most kids haven't mastered the basics and fundamentals. Those things make the game simple and easier. Training is conditioning players to play one on one basketball and not focusing on your strengths. Training should be fine tuning and advance as the player gets better. But kids go from A to Kyrie in one session. One on one basketball is only allowed on the NBA level. It's a long way to get there and a lot of learn- ing along the way. The game doesn't require combo dribble moves, especially when that's not your role. Yes those moves come in handy, but aren't necessary. What the game does require and always will require are the basics and fundamentals.

Now it's good to have those things in your tool box, but learn to be great at something, rather than mediocre at everything. If you're a shooter, master shooting and then learn how to pass. One of the biggest team weak- nesses that coaches take advantage of on the lower lev- els, is the lack of ball handling. Teams will pressure you when they notice that the ball handling is weak. Be pre- pared to get pressed and trapped all game. Coaches preach over and over, beat the press with a pass. It's reasons for that. The ball travels faster than dribbling. I know everyone wants Kyrie Irving handles, but everyone won't get them. His game is more than just handles. It's footwork, timing, touch and heart. Kyrie is another player who has mastered the fundamentals of the game and then made it his. Passing is a part of ball handling and is the most underrated part of the game. Passing is a basic fundamental part of playing basketball. I had all the skills in the world, but I was recruited to play college with a Hall of Fame player, because I could pass him the ball and compete on that level. Everyone has been a role player at some point in their journey. Some early in their career mostly play con- trolled roles, and some later. A controlled role is a strict role when a coach dictates the can and can nots. Don't do this or that, just do your job. Controlled roles can kill confidence or limit development in younger players. Your role is the gateway to your career. Your fit will be

determined by your role. If you're on a team, that team has a need for you. You can find that out by having dialogue with your coach. That's one of the major things you have to do. Find out the coaches expectations and needs. He/she should be transparent with you and able to break it down. When that's clear, that's your focus and concentration area. Do that, which is your role, and win over the coaches' trust. Continue the dialogue and once you gain the trust, you can implement other things, because you delivered on your role, and now the coach will trust the next thing that you will bring to the table if it fits the team. Bring your tool that's needed, but also travel with the whole tool box.

The key is to play. Everyone wants to be in the game. How much, is determined by you. The key to it all, is that you have control over your destiny. You have to create yourself and don't let anyone else determine who or what you are. You come to a coach with something to offer. Even if you don't agree with the coaches perspective of you, that's who or what you are on his/her team. Just think and remember that everything is earned, nothing is given. If you take that approach, you won't have the mental ups and downs worrying about who plays the most, who takes the most shots and those things you can't control. The one thing you do control is you! Be prepared and do your job.

Roles are need based and determined by what you show, or bring to the table. If you come in and show efficiently what your strengths are, you will stand a chance at hav- ing what you do best, be your role. Roles are consistent jobs in sports. When you get to work, you know what your job is. But what's more valuable than your role, is being versatile. Being able to perform multiple roles. Versatility allows you to be whatever a coach needs, whenever he or she needs it. The best way to be this player, starts with mastering the fundamentals and adapting to the game. We spoke earlier on fundamentals and mentioned how Mike Jordan and Kobe Bryant mastered the fundamentals, then made the game theirs. This is the best way to do it. Do it early, because the old- er you get, you set in your ways of comfortability and everyone doesn't respond well to being uncomfortable. Not being able to deal with discomfort during development, is a development killer. If a coach or trainer have you make an adjustment to your footwork or a shot and you don't want to do it because it's uncomfortable, you're slowing the process of your development.

Fundamentals start with the basics, how to play defense, PURPOSE of the triple threat (not the stance), footwork, shooting, passing, boxing out, positioning, basic ball handling and other things you learn in gym class back when it really mattered. Basketball is not taught at gym class anymore, nor do kids play in the park and have older guys to teach them as they go. That's the role the youth coaches have to play. That's what I did. Coaches today put pressure on themselves to win now and find themselves with new teams every year because they don't spend the time to develop what they have. I don't take that approach. Nothing fancy with me, just the correct, simple and basic way to teach the game. I can do that because I know it. Another reason coaches skip the fundamentals today is because players are so athletic. Little do they know, that fundamentals can be the difference that separate you from other players. You can be athletic and super talented, but mastering the fundamentals will make you a smarter and more efficient player. It will also simplify the game. How simple can the game be if you can pass, catch and shoot? Great shooters don't spend time trying to learn dribble combos.

My favorite part of the game will keep you in a coaches rotation on any team. That's VERSATILITY! Even though you have a role, basketball is a situational game that calls for certain players to be in those situations. If a coach needs shooters on the floor, you should be on the floor. If a coach needs the best defensive team out there, you should be on the floor. If the coach needs its best re- bounders or passers, you should be on the floor. Why you should be on the floor? You mastered all of the FUNDAMENTALS and you can do everything right with EFFICIENCY. The coach knows you're going to box out, make strong two hand passes and step into them, play solid defense and help out on rotations. It doesn't take athleticism to do these things. Athleticism is a bonus! Fundamentals get you in the door and helps you earn the trust of a coach. Being a jack of all trades and master of none, will leave you standing with question marks next to your name. What does he or she do best? That's what we all want to know. It's okay to have all the tools in your box that you can go to when needed, but master the one thing that's your strongest talent. It goes back to embracing your strength as your role, and using that to build your confidence and gain the coaches trust. Everybody won't be asked to do everything. You have to be able to show your UNIQUENESS.

Having healthy basketball conversations with older players, different coaches and people around the game, will expand your knowledge of the game and make you a better player. Learning from others will open your mind up while giving you different PERSPECTIVES. You can then formulate your own philosophies and figure out

more about yourself. Shaquille O'Neal said that he didn't get better from the time he spent in the gym, but from

the conversations he had with Bill Russell, Kareem Abdul Jabbar and Pat Riley. We all know that he worked on his game in the gym, but the knowledge, lessons and experience he gained in those conversations, helped advanced him mentally as a player. There is no better teacher than EXPERIENCE. Utilizing the dialogue of players and others around you that have experienced the things that you have seen and have not, will give you better UNDERSTANDING of the game. Talk about the game often and to anybody. Speak your game into existence. CONFIDENCE comes from believing and preparation starts BELIEF. Learn as much as you can, then apply it to the physical work that you have been doing. This stage is one of understanding and finding yourself. Enjoy it in its totality. Embrace its culture, the foundation, the fundamentals and find yourself. Start putting the pieces together and figure out who YOU are as a player and let the EXPERIMENT begin!

"Being true to yourself is the key... It's a sweet justice in knowing that the path you're on, was designed for you and you alone." - Cicely Tyson

Chapter IV:
INTRODUCING...

One of the more fun parts in my basketball life, was when I could compete with the older guys and win. My neighborhood was so competitive that the same team of fives would always play together. It was maybe two teams that would always win. I mentioned earlier that when I use to sit and watch the older guys, I felt that I was a better player than they were. Now that I was acclimated to their game, I was showing it.

Once I established myself as a shooter, they started taking that away by getting out on me quicker and denying me the ball. But I was now comfortable with the speed of the game, because my confidence level was RISING. So all my moves and ball handling tricks, began to work. I settled in and my confidence was sky high. I knew what I was capable of doing, and I did it while I was out there. Still learning from them, because it was so much more, I was now becoming the King of the court.

With development becomes a lot of challenges. You have to continue to work. The better you get, you start to grow a target that gets bigger and bigger and darts start coming from everywhere. Those targets come in many fashions. Harder fouls, tougher defense, more and tougher competition and players who want to prove that they are better than you. When I was first allowed to play, I can remember to start the game, everyone would get a shot at the top of the key, and the first two that make it, are team captains and they get to choose teams. I would never get picked in the first game, and they wouldn't allow me to shoot. They knew that I would make it and play in the first game, so I would have to call next game after the last person in line to play. Some would call next and wait for players who lost in the first game and that would continue. They would keep picking players who just lost because the 10 on the court were the best players. If you wasn't one of those 10, and you got on because you called next, If you lost, you wasn't getting back on the court. You would just watch or go home.

By the time my game would come, the runs were wind- ing down. I would get two good games in if we won the first, and that would be it. Then the lights would be about to come on and the younger kids, younger than me would come on the court just to shoot around and have fun. I would stay up there with them as well. I would be on the court from 3 o'clock when I got out of school playing with my peers, 6 o'clock when the grown men came on after work, and then after they were done with the younger kids until one of my family members would come and get me. I played around the clock. The younger kids didn't play full court games, they played 33 and horse a lot. I would play with them and win all the games, and they would get upset and say i'm to big or to tall. I would ask them if they wanted to play full court. Me against all of them. Didn't matter how many it was, I would play against all the kids out there and it was fun. It was atlas 7-10 every time and I would do this every night. Play 33, Horse then me vs the field. This was where I got my handle from. I had to react so fast and try and keep them from stealing the ball and dribble through, around, through their legs, around their backs every possession. I would get so tired of doing it, but I was getting the ball down court. I was developing my handle and didn't even know it.

The more I played with the older guys, the easier the game got for me. Before you knew it, I was unguardedly and a defenses only hope was to foul me. I went from playing like the 5th or 6th game to getting a chance to shoot for captain. Even then they would make me shoot late, if it lasted that long. But if it did, I was making that shot. It got to a point, another player would ask me to shoot for them and then tell me who to pick after I pick them first. I was in now. I was playing the first game.

Then shortly after that, I didn't have to shoot. I was one of the first picks. This was all between the ages of 12-15. The court was mine! I had figured it out and learned how to play their game. I could compete with the best of the grown men as a teenager. That's when i knew I was really good. They talked about me after the games. I was in the conversation. First I was excited to just sit around them and listen, now i'm in the conversation. That did so much for my confidence and just like a video game, it boosted my ratings.

Now Pandora's Box has opened and you start to see that it's players who are as good as you in other neighbor- hoods near by. Guys start bringing random players to the court just to play against me. I was about 5'11 at the time. When I turned 15 I grew to 6 feet. I was taller than my friends and average around the older guys. I started playing rec ball and I was the center on our team. We started to leave the Neighborhood and going to play against other players on their courts. We didn't lose. We were so competitive and skilled that playing against our age group was a joke. But we would play them because they would challenge us or it was a rec league game.

I grew up playing football and I played while my basket- ball career was starting. I was fully in to football and it has always been my first love. It stopped in High School because I grew in one summer from 6 feet to 6'6. I didn't know any football players that tall, so that ended. I played football at #11 Boys and Girls Club in Washing- ton, D.C. We won the Championship 7 times in 8 years. I was the only one out of my teammates that didn't play basketball for the boys club because I didn't play middle school ball.So one day my friends had basketball practice after we had football practice. So I went in the gym to watch them practice after being invited by my friends. Halfway through the practice, the Coach came over to me and said, "Lonnie, the boys told me you can play." Very calm I told him, "yes I can play." He said, "why aren't you out here?" I told him "I don't know." Then he said come here. I got out the stands and he handed me the ball and said shoot it. I took the ball and shot a jump shot from where I was Standing. My friends were screaming, "I told you!" He got the ball and gave it back and said do it again. I took the ball and shot it again and splash, this one was all nets. He said damn! You're playing. When i stepped on the court to take those shots, I did what he asked. I shot the ball when he gave it to me, while standing a step in front of half court.

I didn't play on that team because I couldn't be at the club that late for practice. I had to walk home after- wards late at night and we use to walk through a lot of alley's to get home. It was about a 20 minute walk. We did it everyday. My first introduction to ORGANIZED basketball was recreation ball. In our area, it was highly competitive. I was blessed to have a few great coaches along the way, Coach Swann, Tim and Ms. Bushrod. Each had their own way of teaching. My first Coach Swann was fun. He made learning the game fun for us. Tim was a little tougher and serious all the time because he was a player himself. He was a must athlete and a re- ally good baseball player. That was his main sport. Ms. Bushrod had basketball swag. She didn't coach in my Neighborhood, she came to get me to play on her version of the dream team. I was teamed up with two of the best players in D.C. Big Hands Eric. They called him hands because he could palm the ball and it looked like an orange in his hands. He was about 6'4 with very long arms as well. He was strong and would dunk on anybody but he had the total package. Petey was about 6'3 and he was as swift as a cat and had a nice jump shot, a slick cross over and he could score fast and in bunches. And then me. I could do it all and along with those two guys, It wasn't fair. After a few games of winning by 40+ points and each of us having 30 points a game, they protested on us because I didn't live in their recreation centers district. But i LEARNED so much from playing with those guys. We were all super talented and any of us could have been called the best, but we were on the same mission and played together and didn't compete against one another. We just played to dominate our opponents.

The word was out around town by then about this skinny kid that goes to Eastern High School that was the truth. All the work that I have been putting in, was now being TESTED. The older guys invited me to play in a grown mens league. I was the youngest player in the league. My Coach, Tim played with me in PICKUP games around the way and put me on the team. Some of the other guys that played out there with us were on this team. Crab, Fred, Big Moonie and my favorite Purple. Purple had just got out of jail and I heard so many stories about him scoring 90 points in jail and averaging about 50 points and i couldn't believe it. The first game we played together, I was amazed at watching him play. He was quick and just played with a different mentality than everyone else. He attacked everything that he did. If he was driving to the basket, he drove as if it was his last drive of the game. He was the real deal. He could dribble (nothing fancy), he could shoot and he could pass really well. He scored about 30 points in the first half. I was a copy cat and soaked up so much whenever I was around the ball.

At the start of the second half, he said young fella I heard about you, it's your turn. I was so eager to impress him, that i played the same way he played. i at- tacked the basket hard, I made jump shots and I played like it was my last game. Afterwards, he looked at me and said, you are as advertised. I was so pumped after this legion gave me a complement. For the rest of the summer, we played together and was recking havoc on opposing teams. I was doing this against grown men. I didn't touch a High School court yet.

After honing your CRAFT, you earn your respect from your peers and you earn your coaches' trust. You have an idea of who you are as a player, while learning from others and EXPERIMENTING. Now you have arrived at the next stage. It's time to show who you are. This is the time to show coaches how your future is shaping up. How you have developed and still DEVELOPING. It's also time for the leader in you to step up. Fundamentals will drive the interest, YOUR game will make the connection fit. Being able to play a fundamentally sound game and adding your game to it, will make you capable of playing any style of basketball, in any SYSTEM and have success doing so. Basketball is a game of stops and makes. Playing defense and putting the ball in the hole is the way to win games. How simple is that? Very simple when you learn how to play the game and play it the right way. It's time to now show off your skill set, your IQ and mental toughness. You are on the leaderboard. You're VO- CAL because you can see and understand the game. You have the EXPERIENCE because you have DISCOV- ERED yourself as a player and you know what you bring to the table. Development never stops, but you are very strong in the things you can do at this point in your career. Now that you are experienced and have a better understanding of the game, you know what's needed and how to develop yourself more into a complete player. You are your best EVALUATOR and trainer, and it started with mastering the fundamentals and learning about yourself.

The most CONFIDENT players become the best leaders. Leaders are able to play the game and make it TRANSLATE to their teammates. Leadership is an important quality because you will affect the mood and soul of the team. All teams must have good leaders. As you developed over the years, one way to lead is to share. All the conversations that you've had, lessons you were taught, share them with your teammates. Have DIALOGUE!

Players today like working out together, that's cool and a good way to bond. Another thing to do is go and have a bite to eat, or sit outside and share basketball stories. Talk about your experiences and the things that are a part of what makes you the player that you are. Talk about your concerns and your greatest attributes. Trust me this level of bonding is game changing and motivational.

All that you have learned over the years will give you all the knowledge to become a great player. Learn from it and LEARN how to apply it! These things will help you manipulate the game. Most kids play today to be good enough to get a video and get likes on a post, that's called "Clout chasing." That's their goals and what they care about the most. They will never say it, but that's what it looks like on the outside looking in. But when you lock in and don't let social media, evaluators and outsiders, be decision makers in the one thing you can control, then you set yourself aside from the rest.

Manipulating the game takes IQ. Knowing what's going on and knowing what everyone is doing on the floor will make you one of the best players on the floor. Being a step ahead of plays and making the proper adjustments on the fly puts you ahead of the game. Having a point guard mindset at any position is an advantage. You don't have to play point guard to think like one. It will make you a better and more VALUABLE player. Next thing is to be a great teammate regardless of the team situation! You want to be the player that everyone can trust and get along with. Your teammates are who you will need to help you manipulate the game. Now you may ask, what does teammates have to do with manipulating the game? Teammates have a lot to do with it.

HERE'S HOW. Number one, you have to skillfully control your teammates. You do this by influencing the situation. When you have your game on point, you're confident, consistent, efficient, and you're a leader, your actions and words speak volume. Younger players will look up to you, older players will follow you and coaches will TRUST you. This is not easy, but it starts with YOU!

"The Key to being successful is having your full concentration. ...having my concentration gives me the confidence to do what I am capable of doing, and be- ing able to be capable of doing what I need to do, comes from practicing what I need to do. " -George "Ice Man" Gervin

Chapter V:
Confidence & Motivation

W E'VE ALL HEARD the word "technician" used in basketball. It's usually to describe a player that's focused on their job. How they approach it, and it's evident by there consistency and efficiency in what it is that they do best. It's that player who knows how to get to his/her spots. Keeps the game simple, fundamentally sound and opens the tool box up when other tools are needed. This should be the goal. KNOWING your job and knowing what you can consistently bring to the table.

When you are performing on a technician's stage, and you now know what you're doing, you know your game and how you can and will contribute to the team, your motivation then becomes your hunger to compete. You're mentally focused and ready, because you've worked so hard to get to this point that you are highly confident and want to share your gifts with the world. I will go a step further, don't mistake your confidence for cockiness, but you want to go and out play whoever you're playing against because you've put the work in and you know you're ready. At this point, you're so locked in that your technical work is flawless. Nobody is perfect, but the only mis- takes will be made will be against good competition. Un- forced turnovers happen, limiting them is a part of maturity. You know yourself, your strengths and your role. You're mature, ready and prepared to bring it! High confidence brings high competitiveness. Once you reach that level of MATURITY, and show mental toughness, all you have left is to do your job. Give it your all and be okay with that. That will always have you in a good clean head space mentally.

Now you can compete on a high level, and set goals for yourself. One of the hardest parts about basketball is to not be comfortable and still be confident in your game. You will have all kinds of negative thoughts and issues holding you back from performing your best. That includes outside people, parents and coaches adding to the mental state of negative thinking. That should not be a factor anymore. You should be the majority owner of your thoughts and your process. Only allow the things that's going to help you GROW remain in your thoughts. Self motivation is key. You can't depend on coaches to motivate you. Even when a coach or teammate try and motivate you, you still have to allow yourself to rise up. I got to a point where I had to motivate myself before games. When I would stand at the circle for jump ball, I would stand there and wait for a player to say they're guarding me. "I got number twenty one." I would take that as disrespect. In my head I would say to myself, why did he choose me? Is he crazy? I'm about to give him the business." Then I would say to him, "your coach must not like you if he told you to guard me. Or you're just crazy." That would start it for me. An instant heated competition as soon as the ball went up.

Another way to challenge yourself, is to set in game goals. Remember first that it's a team game. Don't set goals outside of what the team needs to get accomplished. No player has ever become great alone. Some goals for example would be, defensively getting 3 stops in a row, playing great help defense, grab 5 defensive rebounds or whatever you can add to help you always stay locked in. Offensively, however many assist you think is possible. If you're really good, play with more left hand possessions than right. I loved playing with my left hand in summer league games. I even played with my left against pros. I would play a whole game shooting with my left hand. Making left handed passes, dribble with my left and be efficient. Whatever it takes, you have to motivate you!

When you start to feel like a ball player and your walk changes then people start to recognize you, they tell you good things that are basketball related, it's a great feel- ing that makes you want to be even better. Now the road to greatness all depends on your maturity, discipline and sacrifice. Whenever you want to take it to the next level, you have to use the same development process and do what that level is doing. It's similar to learning the fundamentals. It's always a way to play and a style of play each level you go up. Remember each time you go up, you begin again. TRANSITIONING from middle School to High School, High School to College, College to professional, it's all a different game. You have to learn each game when you get there.

WITHIN EACH LEVEL there are sub levels. Middle school has sixth, seventh, 8th grade. High school has Freshman, Sophomore, Junior and Senior. Then Professional has rookie and you continue to grow each year after. Development never stops. I'll say that again, DEVELOP- MENT NEVER STOPS! The good thing about growth is that it makes you feel good. That good feeling is a part of confidence. Now you add all the things you've learned together and go for broke. At this stage in my life, I was unstoppable. In Middle School, I played more recreation ball than anything, but I played ball every day and I was on the court every night until I had to go home. I fell in love with the game. In High School, my Senior year, I was one of the most skilled players in the area. I shot a high field goal percentage, close to 68% and most of my shots were mid ranged jumpers and threes. But my real skill came out when I would play in the local leagues with the older players. I was allowed to do more. Mentally because I was having success against these players, my confidence was through the roof.

MY TEENAGE YEARS, my mindset was different. I believed that I was the best player walking, and I played like it. To get to this point, I played a lot of basketball my way. My skills and my IQ all matched the level of my confidence. My cousin would give me challenges to keep me engaged and locked in every game. One game he would say, drive to the whole and get at least ten dunks. An- other game he would say get five assists with your left hand, and another five with your right. And as I mentioned before, he would tell me to play the first half with your left hand, or the whole game. I was doing this against NBA players in a league called the Urban Coalition, and doing it well. I was UNSTOPPABLE.

Highly confident is where you should be after putting the work in. There should be no other way. Your reason for playing shouldn't be to gain a scholarship, it shouldn't be for social media likes, videos or clout. It should be because you LOVE the game. When you love the game, you will get what you deserve from it. What happens when you love something? You go all out for it. You give it your all, because it's what you revere the most. That should be your motivation, your driver and your why. Your love for the game should be your motivation! That is greatness PERSONIFIED.

Success is determined by you. Not if you're ranked or all American. That's someone's opinion and a little politics. Success is; giving something you love your all, and being fine with the OUTCOME. It's your happiness gained through the things that you're passionate about. Basketball should be that to you. When you're in between the courts line, the game is yours. Yes you have teammates, coaches and competitors, but nothing is stopping you from giving your all. You should want to give your all if you're prepared. Preparation has to be smart and disciplined. It's time to refine and tune your skills. Study the game, watch films of yourself and players that you admire and games that you model yours after. The process repeats itself. You can get better as long as you play the game. Your body may change, and your mind can continue to grow. Find ways to make it work for you. You have the tools and the mentality to be successful. When you know something, you're confident. Know your game.

Translation: taking something from one phase to another.

Chapter VI:
TRANSLATION

IN LIFE, WE want all the work that we put in to TRANS- LATE to the things we want to accomplish. How do we take our trainings and preparation and make it trans- late to the game? What's the PROCESS like to see the fruits of your labor? To answer these questions, and to get a different PERSPECTIVE than my own, I've spoken to a lot of players about their training and workouts, to get a better understanding of how others feel about basketball training, and how it translates to the game. I found some interesting perspectives on this topic from players, coaches and parents.

One of the more popular answers by professionals across multiple sports PLATFORMS, was that they train to stay in shape and to stay SHARP. Now this is one of the greatest MISPERCEPTIONS in training. It is popular for some to go on YouTube or social media and see what the professionals are doing and try to EMULATE it. When you see Steph Curry warming up before games, you see him doing some fancy ball handling drills with two balls and shooting deep shots. How are his pregame workouts getting him better? How will they get YOU better? He's already an exceptional ball handler and shooter. His arsenal is already full and he knows how to use his tools. These are things that he has already MASTERED. Thats how he warms up and gets his RHYTHM before games. He's not doing those things to get better in that moment. He's one of the best ball handlers and players in the game. He warms up to jump start his rhythm and his feel for his hands and the ball. When I see trainers teaching kids stuff that NBA players are doing, it seems to me that they're teaching moves that have no significant purpose to help develop in to a better PLAYER. It's show work. Work that makes you look good but not a better player. I understand both sides because I had the fundamentals, IQ and I could put on a show. NBA players are very good players, and everything they do is CALCULATED. Young persons who haven't mastered the fundamentals, shouldn't be spending the majority of their time working on moves that NBA players do. Focus should be on LEARNING how to play the game. If a player hasn't mastered the fundamentals, FUNDAMENTAL skill training should be your main focus. Some players are exceptional and you can teach them those advanced moves if they have an understanding of the game.

COACHES AND TRAINERS shouldn't have 10 kids in training sessions and have all 10 doing the same moves unless it's fundamental basketball drills. Players have different skill levels and different NEEDS. Group training should be basic and focused on fundamentals. Another way is live ACTION pickup games and teaching them the game as you go. I've had more player development success teaching the game rather than training and working on moves. Five on five free play or pickup games, allows me to watch every player and how they react and respond to the game. I can see their natural instincts, what works for them and how to develop those things and working on the weaknesses that were revealed while playing. We have to remember when we are developing players, the goal is to teach the game. We want to make them the best players they can be. Even if it's a role, players have to master their roles. That doesn't mean their games can't evolve, it just means they have to master something. Be. great at something. That's the consistent thing that will take you a long way. Everyone can't lead a team in scoring and it's not team ball trying to out score your teammate. I learned early that I had teammates who were better scorers than I was even if I was the best player.

Some trainers will promote their style of teaching by telling you that this PROFESSIONAL player does this to get better. Those are not the things that PROS did to become better players. In fact, there are no drills that will make you a better in-game player. Drills help to DE- VELOP and refine skills. It's a totally different category from playing the game. That's where the distinction line should be drawn between skill development and "in game IQ". What skills TRANSLATES to the game? Your IQ is the #1 answer. The higher your IQ, the better player you are regardless of your skill set. To have your skills and IQ ALIGNED, you will become a really good player. Greatness will come if you have that level of great workout ethic. Great players are just different from others because they know it and they show it. It's not something talked about. It's in your effort and actions.

IQ IS UNDERSTANDING the game of basketball. But what is it to understand? It sounds simple, but there is so much to LEARN in the game. Every coach you play for will teach you something different. Learn it, don't ignore it. Pay attention to every DETAIL being taught. Even the details have details. Learning how to use a screen is a broad topic. It's so many ways to come off a screen and there are many different kinds of screens. So the details are a must. Players are all different although some have similarities. Physical traits can make you different. Speed, quickness, strength and IQ can make the difference on how you use screens. Coaches are doing their best to try and teach you things that translate that you will experience in the game. Regardless of how good a coach is, it's so much more to be taught and so many details into understanding the game. There are always lessons to learn from different prospectives.

Knowing is the mental preparation to prepare you for the things you need to do to be successful in games. You can have the best dribbling skills in the world. But if you don't have the IQ, or mental understanding of the game, you will not be as successful as you can be. IQ is knowing why to go pick and roll, how to read the pick and roll, what the pick and roll will cause and the effect of the pick and roll. Skill developing is, how to dribble over the pick, splitting the pick and attacking or shooting off the pick. How does this translate to the game? #1, the pick and roll is not for every player. That's where your role comes in to play. Regardless if you can dribble, If you don't have the IQ, you will just run off the pick like you were taught in training. The pick and roll is an art form. I figured that out In 1996, when I was invited by Coach Pat Riley to workout for the Miami Heat. It was only 4 players at the workout and I was the only player that was not a returning player on the Miami Heats 1995 roster. Coach Riley had us defending the pick and roll and doing the pick and roll everyday for the whole week I was there. I had never ran the pick and roll so much in my short career at the time. If i didn't understand it be- fore I got there, I understood it when I left. I had never played point guard at the time and the Heat had 3 older Point Guards on their roster. Tim Hardaway, Gary Grant and John Crotty. I didn't know the purpose of the workout, I was the only ball handler doing it over and over until I was blue in the face, also while doing Pat Riley's "Sprint Test" each day before and after we worked out. It was one of the hardest workouts I had ever had. But i learned so much and became a better player in one week.

I didn't understand when I reached the pro level, why all the interested teams had me working out as a Point Guard. It was so much more than being able to dribble. I found out later that it was because i played with a high IQ and I could create scoring for other players. That part of my game was natural. I was a play maker. I was fortunate enough to get to talk to Coach Riley and listen to him give me the anatomy of the pick and roll as he jogged on the treadmill which seemed forever. He taught me so much during that week that I became a "true" Point guard from his teachings. I had the skills, but he gave me the know how. The mental game. Changed my thought process and also taught me that I could be a point guard from any position on the court.

When you hear feedback of why you're not doing things in the game that you have been working on in training, It's because you're not training for the game. It get's real with 9 other players on the floor. Your visuals are differ- ent, your space is different, the defense is different. Now, how the training can actually translate is the muscle memory of the actions you learn while simulating the fundamentals of the game. Fundamentals are a basic form of basketball. They can help you survive while you develop other aspects of the game. Fundamentals are a time buyer as you develop your skills, strength, speed and other things that help you become a better physical competitor. Trainers have to do their due diligence as well. Every player has a role on a team. Not everyone is going to handle the ball and be able to do dribble moves they spend hours working on with trainers and coaches.

TRAINERS HAVE TO get out and see what the players can do and are allowed to do on their teams. Coaches have to actually scout players and also know what they are capable of. Learn their comfort zones and where their spots are on the floor. Once you figure that out, then you train and teach game specific things in those areas and strengths. You will see the translation from the work- outs to the game. Translation is also a mental part of the game.Training has been diluted from its original purpose. Families, coaches and trainers, have made it "the thing to do," in- stead of the thing that makes you better. I watch videos on social media of kids training and highlights. They get you excited and interested in seeing these players play. Then when you see a player live, you're disappointed because most of them don't know how to play the game. They don't play how you were expecting. Training should be about fundamental skill development and game simulation. The game simulation is what i mentioned earlier about coaches and trainers evaluating their players strengths and building on that by helping them with the things that they're involved in on the court the most. The shots available to them, defensive positioning, different passing angles, where they are more valuable for the team. Those are the things to build on and develop the player. These things grow confidence. When a player begins to play with more confidence and understand the game, you can teach them anything. Remember, don't leave out defense and boxing out. Those are two of the most overlooked fundamentals of the game.

Development has come to a point for me, where I can tell a kid, go slap the wall 3 times with your left hand, then next play down, make that post entry pass with your left hand. They may have never made that pass before or uncomfortable making it, but because I have showed them so many other things that have worked, they trust me and buy into the things that i am teaching. Our relationship, confidence and trust has grown between us, which makes teaching easier. Those are the ingredients to player development. Not many at this level can say they had the chance to workout and play with Michael Jordan, Kobe Bryant, Allen Iverson, Mitch Richmond, Alonzo Mourning, Vince Carter, Grant Hill, Dennis Scott, Penny Hardaway, Baron Davis, Derek Anderson and many more to name a few. As well as being coached by John Thompson, Bryan Hill, Darryl Dawkins, Eric Musselman, Larry Brown and Dave Leitao. The things i've learned, the conversations i've had and the experience gained has put me in a position to share and produce results.

The way I developed my game was unorthodox, not typical. But it gave me my own perspective of the game. It showed me that I could be whatever type of player, whenever I needed to be. I was so far beyond my years, that during my prime, I was misunderstood. Although I shot a high percentage of 30 foot jump shots, coaches weren't comfortable with that. I would pull up on the fast break with an opportunity for a layup and shoot the three. I shot runners from the three point line, even shot left handed threes. I was an excellent ball handler and passer. Basketball was fun and I played it fast. But it was developed through playing, working at it and confidence. Everything I have done was worked on against real defense before It was done in a game. I played so much ball, that the only difference a game made was the game plan. I competed hard and played to win regard- less where I was playing.

Watching the NBA today, seeing Kevin Durant, Luka Doncic, Kyrie Irving, Steph Curry and others, I was 6'8 doing the things they are doing, in the 80's and 90's. It was appreciated by the fans and a lot of veteran players and coaches. But on the higher levels, most coaches couldn't accept it. I am settled with my career and all of my experiences and the talent I was blessed with. My experiences are meant for me to share with the future of the game. Through it all, I gave it my all and I'm fine with that. I've had a lot of help along the way, I learned so much from so many others games, and made all that I learned my own. I put the time in, I worked smart, I worked hard, I figured it out, I developed myself! I put the work in, I listened, I studied and I decided that basketball was my life. When people ask why I'm not in the NBA I tell them it wasn't for me. I had two opportunities to play in the league. The first one I got injured and the second one I didn't pass the physical. That's when I knew I had a different calling. But i've learned so much and have experienced so much with great coaches and players, that today those things have influenced me to teach and share.

Translation is a part of the development process most can't figure out. It's like the advertising business. You see a commercial and the object being sold is such a beauty, but when you experience it for yourself, it's not what you expected. We watch our players workout then we wonder why we're not seeing these things from the workouts in the game. Nobody can control that but the player. If the player does not have the confidence, or trust and believe what they're being taught, it will not work. My reason why I take the blame for developing myself, is that I learned so many things from so many players and coaches, that I was willing to do the work and better myself when I had the time to do it alone. I never had a trainer to tell me how to do it. I watched, listened and studied the game. I wanted it for myself so I created myself.

A basketball career is a very tricky in the sense that it's not for everyone to be the greatest ever, or play at the highest level. So many factors have control over your ending as far as your career. Number one, if it's God's will, you will have all that you dream of. The only thing you have control over is your game. When you under- stand your game and your style, you have to watch the teams that you are interested in laying for, and see how you fit. Not all the time you fit on a team because you're a really good player. Even with being a versatile player and able to adapt to any environment, coaches will al- ways have their own perception of you. If you play for a coach who don't play your style, you can't expect your game to translate in that coaches system. I was a victim of that. The New York post wrote an article in 1992 that talked about this. The objective of the article was about Allen Iverson playing the most minutes as a Freshman in the history of Georgetown basketball. Rightfully so because Iverson was a very special player and became an NBA Hall of Fame player. In that article, the writer asked a question about another Freshman who he felt should have played more, and that freshman was me.

"Thompson has been known to suppress the playing time and the exuberance of his youngest hot shots. He doesn't let them talk to the press for a large chunk of their freshman year, and they are also supposed to restrain themselves from self-expression while at- tired in shorts and sneakers. "Lonnie's a very good shooter, once he gets a lot of the Boogaloo out of his game," Thompson once said of a hot-shot freshman named Lonnie Harrell (after Harrell's 3-pointer had helped beat Connecticut, it should be noted.) The word Boogaloo seemed to imply helter-skelter, down- home, run-and-gun offensive tactics not in vogue at the 206-year-old university in the leafy corner of the District of Columbia." - George Vecsey, NY Times 1995

Although I had the fundamentals, perception is everything. My style of play was seen as playground basket- ball and was not appreciated because of the flash. I remembered when John Thompson told me at practice one day that my game was pretty just by playing hard and I didn't have to do anything flashy. But flashy to him was a dribble between the legs, a crossover or behind the back by a tall player. I was 6'6 at the time and played a fast pace game having multiple skills that I could do these things running full speed. It made me a really hard to defend player. I was a good piece to a team that had a really good floor general in Joey Brown, one of the most dominate big men in the country in Alonzo Mourning and a young team that had the potential to go a long way in the NCAA tournament. Some have said I was the missing piece because the years before me, Georgetown was a defensive focused team that always had good big men leading the team, but didn't have that offensive player that opened the floor up since Reggie Williams and Charles Smith. It was Alonzo Mournings senior year and I could have been that player. It just seemed the way that I played, I was ahead of my time and I played for a Hall of Fame Coach, that wasn't ready for a player like me at that time. Even accepting my role on the team and doing the things I was asked to do, I was the same flashy player (in his mind) he called

"Boogaloo."

"The man who has no imagination, has no wings." - Muhammed Ali

Chapter VII:
Dreams & Visions

ON SATURDAY'S AND Sunday's in the 80's, only a few NBA teams would be nationally TELEVISED. It was the 4 teams with the most popular players in the League at the time. The Los Angeles Lakers, Boston Celtics, Philadelphia 76'ers and the Detroit Pistons. Very few games were televised because TV sitcoms were more popular at the time. Even during the NBA playoffs, the Friday night playoff games would be tape DELAYED because Friday nights were primetime for TV. "Dallas" the TV series was the most popular show on primetime TV, so the earlier games would come on later that night at 11:30pm. I use to watch every game that came on and I was a big fan of George "ICE MAN" Gervin. That was the first player introduced to me by my uncle. He bought me the iconic a poster of Ice Man sitting on the Ice blocks in his silver sweatsuit palming two basketballs. He didn't get a lot of TV time in y region, but when he did, my uncle would let me know to watch. I watched so much that i begun to understand the game. I loved the Philadelphia 76'ers, Magic Johnson, and Larry bird. I didn't like the Detroit Pistons because of their bad boy IMAGE. These were the teams and players that we saw the most on TV during the weekends.

When the school week would begin, I would go to School and talk with my friends about the games and the moves we saw our FAVORITE players doing. As soon as school ended for the day, we would rush to the courts and imagine that we were those players and do the moves we saw them doing all week long. We would pre- tend to be those players and race to call out which play- er we were going to IMITATE first. "I'm Magic," I would hurry and yell out before anyone else could. That meant when we played, i had to throw the fancy no look PASSES like i saw Magic do and his moves. This would be a full week of IMAGINING that we were those players. We DREAMED about being great like them.

IMAGINATION was such a huge part of our DEVELOPMENT growing up. We would copy the players we saw and do their moves just like the way we saw them do it. All week long, we would perfect these moves, until the next game, then try something else we saw a player do. This is where imagination meets REAL life. On our BASKETBALL courts that we played on every day, we became our favorite players. Whether it was two of us or ten of us, we pretended to be those GREAT players! Our imaginations grew every week until we started actually feeling like we were them. It got to a point when others would see us play and say, you play just like Magic Johnson. One of my friends name was Mike, and Michael Jordan was his favorite player. He walked like Mike, had his sneakers and could play just like him. We were that GOOD!

When we began to become better players, our imaginations grew bigger and BIGGER. We started seeing our- selves as PROFESSIONAL athletes and started playing as if we were. Our imaginations did a lot for our confidence and maturity as players. During that time, we would dominate other kids our age. We felt we were pros for real. Our ego's and confidence really had us playing on a higher level than our peers. It's so important to want to be GREAT. You set a bar for yourself in sports and you do your best to reach it. You have plenty of players before you to give you the MOTIVATION and blueprint to reach your GOALS. A part of that is seeing yourself there before you actually get there. "Fake it til you make it,'" was a saying people use to say when a person was to act as if they are something they're not.

When you have the ASPIRATIONS and put in the work to get there, it makes sense. Imagining and living in your SUCCESS before you experience it works the same way. When you're working out, you have to imagine your DOMINATION, imagine making those game winning PLAYS, imagine hitting those game winning SHOTS, because trust me when the time comes, it will feel natural. You have to ENVISION yourself in situations and imagine you are the player that you want to be. It came a time when I was a professional player, that when I was faced with a situation that was clutch, I was CONFIDENT, because it felt like I was there before. I was excited rather than being nervous. That confidence and the positive energy it exudes, would allow me to make the big shots. Nobody's perfect. You can't make them all, but when the situation approaches, you'll be the first one to say, Coach, give me the BALL!

Imagination is EVERYTHING. You're practicing for your big day. You're putting yourself in POSITION to accomplish your goals. You're PLANTING your own seeds. Figuring out who you want to be as a player starts with your imagination. How can you become it if you don't VISUALIZE it? Your youth trainers and coaches should help you get to your goals as a player. They should know where you see yourself heading as a player, and they should help you get there. SHARE your vision with those who are assisting in your development. Your visions have to be realistic. You also have to be willing to put the WORK in to get where you want to go. Your imagination works along with your FAITH. Faith are things hoped for that are yet not seen. When you have vision, you're exercising faith. But faith with- out works is DEAD. You have to put the work in to get the results you want.

I've always had a BIG IMAGINATION. I played football and imagined that I was my favorite football player from the Los Angeles

Rams, Eric Dickerson. When I played, I did it as if I was him. When playing basketball, I did the same things. I ran the floor in TRANSITION and passed like Magic Johnson. I wanted to shoot like Larry Bird. But as I got older, I MASTERED changing into whatever player I needed to be that game. I was able to do that be- cause I worked on my all around game by taking things away from the players I LIKED the most. I would do the things I'd taken from them when i played pickup. I had an all around game. Even years later my DEFENSE had gotten better from watching Scottie Pippen use his length. When i finally became a pro, I was asked to de- fend the best player REGARDLESS of the position and I was up for the challenge. I wanted to guard the best player anyway because I wanted him to guard me back so he could see he wasn't better than me. That was how competitive I was.

In the Summer of 2002, I played at RUCKER PARK in New York City with an imaginative mindset that nobody knew about. Nobody had an idea of what they were watching really but me. All they knew was that they were watching "The Prime Objective." PRIME OBJEC- TIVE was the nickname that was given to me at Rucker Park by MC Hannibal. I wanted them to see me play and enjoy watching me compete and entertain. At the time, it wasn't a player like myself in New York that was 6'8 in height, playing with the instincts and shooting ability I had. I was built to except the challenges and be a MISMATCH for smaller guards and players my size or bigger. I could play above the rim and shoot it as deep as half court with dazzling ball handling SKILLS. What I added to that, was wearing jersey #8 and channeling Latrell Sprewell. Sprewell use to run the floor RELENT- LESSLY and attack the rim like a savage. So while I was playing, I would play my game, but whenever I was on the break or driving to the basket, I imagined that I was Sprewell. It made me UNSTOPPABLE and one of the most talked about players all across the country for the next few summers.

I always have used my imagination to further my VERSATILITY on the court. When I was younger playing Center, I remembered watching Danny Manning at Kansas and how he lead his team as being a big, and one of the PRIMARY ball handlers. I use to watch how David Robinson would turn and face at Navy, and although I wasn't a fan, I was also curious of why Bill Lambeer of the Detroit Pistons was shooting long jump shots and he was one of the biggest players on the court. A lot of CURIOSITY goes with imagination. Wanting to know all about the game and wanting to be great makes you very curious.

There is no QUICK way to wake up in the morning, wanting to be a great basketball player and just become it without putting in the WORK. A lot of players were born with God given TALENT and ability, but even they have to FIGURE out how to use those talents. Wanting to know why Michael Jordan was so good and how did he become it, is being curious. I watched him play and LISTENED to his interviews and got an idea of how he was so SUCCESSFUL. One thing that always RES- ONATES with me about Mike is that he always mentions his work ETHIC. When someone talks, listen to them. We all know how TALENTED Mike was, but when you start to look at the game differently with the curiosity of becoming a great player, you start to pay attention to MANNERISMS and how players react and figure out why they made a move or defensive play. Watching Mike and hearing him always talk about his work ethic, I started NOTICING how he never took a play off. He played with the same intensity on offense and defense. I watched how hard he ran in TRANSITION from offense to defense. How his first step was big and long when he fought around screens. How quick he changed directions on defense and how he ACCELERATED whenever he ATTACKED. It was non-stop and he didn't take BREAKS in between plays. That was the work ethic he spoke about. So I played with that in mind. That was one of the LESSONS learned from being curious.

I've played with so many great players over the years, but one player stood out MORE than others. He was the SMALLEST player, but had the biggest heart. It was the Summer of 1995 and we were playing pickup at George- town University. I was playing on a team with Allen Iverson and we were out there having FUN. He was rapping Biggie versus and I was laughing while we were playing. We were playing against a team that had Dan Marjle, Alonzo Mourning and Patrick Ewing on it. A lot of PROS use to come and play with us when they were in town in D.C. during the summers. We've had, Charles Barkley, Magic Johnson and many more, including all of the former Georgetown alumni that had became professionals. The games were 5 on 5 full court and very PHYSICAL. The pros were there to stay in shape and also give out LESSONS in the form of being physical and letting you know the DIFFERENCE between levels. But this game didn't go in their FAVOR. Allen was so quick and fast, and couldn't be GUARDED and everybody knew that. I was crafty with the ball and an EXCELLENT passer. I could get the ball to anybody anywhere on the court. What was so IMPRESSIVE to me was how Allen would ATTACK the basket and challenge both Alonzo Mourning and Patrick Ewing and finish. This guy is 6 feet tall and was winning at the rim against a 7 foot- er and a 6'9 DEFENSIVE beast. I just kept watching him to try and figure out how and why. Again I was curious. This curiosity occurred while we were playing together. It's one thing watching from the SIDELINES and another watching on the same floor in real TIME.

One of the things that i noticed was his triple threat. It goes unnoticed and it wasn't the basic triple threat that you're taught in basic fundamental basketball. He was so low to the ground and had long arms and would square up in a position to let you know he was going by you. His arms was long and the ball would be below him almost touching the floor. In this position, it's no way you could body him and take away his space. If you tried, his first dribble would be by you and it would be his body against your 1 leg. That was a fundamental move, that was overlooked because people were so amazed by his crossover. All the great ones have fundamentals and know the basics. It may not look like what you are taught, but you have to know them to understand how the game is played. Everything I witnessed and liked, I would take it and use it in a game the same way I saw the player use it. I'm 6'8 so I didn't expect A.I.'s triple threat to work for me the same. The next time I played pickup, i used it. I used it the whole game in various ways to see how it could work for me. To my surprise, it worked! It gave me an advantage be- cause of my length and my first step. i never did the basic triple threat again. I had to be smart, because you couldn't always shoot from that position if someone jammed you. So you had to be smart and use it in the right situation.

I also watched his confidence and how he knew in his mind that he was unstoppable. It's one thing to think it, and another to know it! He knew it. You could just see that he was in a mental place that nobody else on the court mattered to him. He moved around the court loosely as if the game had no rules. He would gamble on defense and do it all out, and make the plays. He would split defenders and find his teammates and make some of the most amazing passes. He would finish plays over the bigs at the rim and it looked like it happened in slow motion. They were at his mercy, almost to the point they couldn't foul him how they wanted to. It was so inspiring to watch it and he showed me the advantages of being a small player with a big heart. You have to be skilled and have a big heart to be as successful as he was. A.I. had all of the fundamentals and basics with his style on top.

It falls in place with learning the game and making it your own. The things I saw him do I added to my game and made it my own. But his biggest skill or talent, was his confidence. I've spent two years with A.I. in Philadelphia. We would be in the front of a hotel just hanging out and he would pull a ball out of the trunk and say let me see something. He wanted to see the new moves from the DC area. At the time, a very popular move that was mastered by Pol- ish, T-Roy, Greg Jones, Moochie Norris and Lorenzo, we called it, "the hands up" or just "HANDS" for short. It was the way we would do a hesitation and dip our bodies like we were ready to shoot and even bring the hand that we wasn't dribbling the ball with up to the ball like we were about to grab it and shoot. You had to have good ball control because to hesitate and pause your dribble without carrying was the challenge. When he did it, he added it to his crossover, because the way we did it, looked awkward when he did it. We just laughed at the attempt. We would be fully dressed to hang out, dribbling a basket ball and sharing and talking about moves. It was in our veins. Regardless of the place or time, we would be talking about basketball. We would go even as far as how we would do a defender if one was guarding us and demonstrating it.

I spent a lot of time playing ball with the locals and other NBA players in Philly as well. Some of the best runs were at Augustine Lake. Philly greats like Eddie Jones, Mark Jackson, Catino Mobley, Alvin Williams, Aaron McKie and even 76ers players like Larry Hughes would be there to play. I went to play all the time. A.I. would pop in a few times when he had the time. By then, I was accepted as a an official pro. I have played against most of these guys already in the Bakers league. That was my first introduction to Philadelphia basketball. I traveled up from DC the summer after my senior year in college, I wanted to test my skills in another pro league outside of DC's Urban Coalition.

ONE OF MY mentors at the time, was friends with The Director of the Bakers league Sunny Hill. He told him about me and Sunny said bring him up. While I was in College, I use to dream about going city to city and dominating every court I played on. My friends in school would talk about the leg- ends and the greats in their areas and I would sit there thinking in my mind, your hood hasn't seen me yet. When I got the opportunity to travel and play in differ- ent cities, I made sure I approached it that way and left my mark. That game I played in Philly was against, Bob- by Phils (RIP), Eddie Jones, Aaron McKie, Pooh Allen and Rick Mahon to name a few. These were some well known NBA players and defenders. But before I got the chance to play against them, the first game I showed up for, the coach didn't know me and he wouldn't play me. I sat on the bench the whole game in a tight small yellow uniform that had me looking like a Yellow stick figure. We were down 20 and Sunny Hill said to the coach, "put the new kid in and see what he got. You don't have nothing to lose." He still didn't want to put me in. Finally in the fourth quarter, the game is over and we're down 30, he throws me in. I was so excited as if the game just started. We were down 30 and I helped us cut it to 15 by scoring 20 points in the quarter. When the game ended, the coach ran to me as if we won and said, "you have to come back next week." I told him I will be here. He asked did I know anyone else that can play like me? I told him yes. I went on to score 40 points in the first half before injuring my Achilles on the first play of the 2nd half that next game against the NBA players mentioned. They were the best team in the league and stacked with talent. This was one of my best games and what made it so great, was that on the drive up, I said I was going for 50. Moochie Norris Washington D.C. Sursum Quarters native, NBA player and one of DC's finest, was the player I chose to take the trip wit me. He was my favorite play- er from our area and the way he played the game, fit my style perfect. He played fast, had a high IQ and could get me the ball when I'm open and still get his. It was a no brained to take him with me.

I made thirteen three point shots out of 15 in that first half, and he probably assisted on everyone. The rest of the points came against double teams and making crazy shots. Things I have already done before. I played in this game before. I imagined the whole outcome. I put myself in these games before I actually played in them. That was my comfort zone. I loved the big stage. I loved the competition. I was BRED for it. The conversations and creating the situations in my mind, and imagining the outcomes, have created the blueprint for me to ACTIVELY accomplish my goals. Mental development is as important as physical. You have to imagine where you're go- ing and really see yourself being there and put in the WORK to get there. The majority of the things that I have done, I mapped it out in my head first, sometimes during the game as well. It helped my CONFIDENCE and it helped my game.

OUR DREAMS AND visions are what drives us. We all have things that we ASPIRE to achieve. If we want them bad enough, we will do the things NECESSARY to have them. It starts with a little FAITH and believing and knowing we can ATTAIN them if we put in the work. We have to have vision and see it MANIFEST. Muhammed Ali once said,

> "Champions aren't made in gyms. Champions are made from something they have deep inside of them a desire, a dream, a vision. They have to have the skill, and the will. But the will must be stronger than the skill."

That is our code. It's that something inside of us that we all have, we create it with our minds. We have to put in the work to make it actually happen. That's who we are, and that's who we shall be.

"CLUTCH"

Chapter VIII:
Clutch Gene
(Bred to react, it's something you can't teach)

I REMEMBER THE time I took and made my first game winning shot. I had never been in a SITUATION where my team NEEDED a last second shot in a playoff game. It was a play that was drawn up during the time out and it was win or go home. I was playing in South Dakota for the Rapid City Thrillers during the NBA lockout season in the ABA. I've made big shots before, but never a buzzard beater to win the game. It was 3 seconds left, I remember running to the bench first when coach called timeout and said, "GIVE me the ball." My team was full of scorers, so I wanted to get the last shot before he made his mind up and drew up the play. My teammates trusted me, I also trusted them, but I just wanted to PLANT that seed because coach could have given it to anyone. We were that TALENTED as a team.

The ball was being inbounded at half court. I told my coach to get me the BALL at the top of the key. He said ok and drew up the play. It was only THREE seconds left, it was enough time to pump FAKE and take a dribble to get the shot off if I needed to. But I KNEW that spot like the back of my hand. I told them, just get me the ball, this is MONEY. I already knew that in my head, because I have made this shot so many times at home on my CREATED baskets growing up, and on the playground in a lot of PICKUP games.

AS WE WALKED out of the timeout, I told the inbound passer, to get me the ball as soon as I cleared the screen. I knew that if I got the ball, i would make the shot. My MIND was made up. I BELIEVED that. When I was on my home courts as a youngster, I would imagine myself being at the LA Great Western Forum. I would be playing for the Lakers and we would be down 1 with 10 seconds left to win the championship. I would count down from 10. Cooper inbounds it to Magic, TEN...NINE... EIGHT...SEVEN...SIX...FIVE...FOUR Harrell comes off the screen, Magic passes it to Harrell, THREE...TWO... ONE... he shoots, IT'S GOOOOOD!!! Lonnie Harrell hits the game WINNER of the NBA Championship. I would make the shot and jump up and down and celebrate as if I just won. These moments TRANSLATED mentally to the court. When I would play full court games with my friends, the games would go to thirty two with all two point shots. I would always take the LAST shot. It was no clock, but in my mind, I would always imagine that last shot as a game winning moment, bigger than the MOMENT I was actually taking the shot. I would remember shots taken by the pros and do what I saw them do. I would tell myself I was Larry Bird sometimes, because I seen him take big shots a lot. I would put myself in those MOMENTS. No matter the setting, the last shot was mine and it was always a must make and a big thing to me. My CONFIDENCE was sky high.

WHEN MY MOMENT came, It wasn't expected, but I was ready for it. We set up for the play. I was on the low block opposite the inbound passer who was the Point Guard. Opposite box from me was the other guard that could shoot. At the top of the key was one post player and on the low block stacked with the other guard was the other post player. When the ref handed the inbound passer the ball, I ran toward the stack, as if i was going off the screen. Once I started, the other shooter ran to the ball side corner, the post player in the stack, ran to the free throw line. He met the other post and they set an elevator door screen for me. I faked and cut hard to get to the elevator. Once I got through, my defender was trailing me and the elevator screen closed. I saw him coming, but all I wanted to do was catch the ball then make something happen. When I caught the ball at the top of the key, the pass was on time but my back was to the

basket. I saw the defender coming, and he was hustling around the elevator screen after it had closed. I caught the pass and in one motion, took a dribble away from the 3 point line, picked the ball up and turned in the air and shot a one legged fadeaway. The ball was in the air, I heard teammates voices, but couldn't make out what they were saying, and my coach screaming "noooooo" until the shot went in all net. They were jumping and celebrating and ran on the floor as the buzzard went off. I just responded as If i just made another shot. I was talking in a low tone to myself, saying, "that's what I do."

I didn't have the personal response or the joy that I thought i would after making a big shot in the pros. I've made big shots in college and in other leagues. But this time I had a chip on my shoulder. It was a big game and it was win or go home. I was CHALLENGING myself to be great in this moment. I thought I was doubted by my coach screaming "no," when I shot the deep fadeaway. For him It was about taking a GOOD balanced shot hav- ing your feet set. And for me it was about just getting the shot off and being CONFIDENT knowing that it was go- ing in. It was a shot that he had seen me take before, but not the shot he thought I should take in that moment. That was understood, but for me, I knew that shot. It was about getting the ball off. He understood it when we talked about it and I told him that I took that shot with the same urgency and confidence I take all my shots. I never chuck a shot up and hope it goes in. I shoot to make every shot that I take as if it's my last.

A lot of big plays are made in the mind before they actually happen. Being clutch is not a perfect thing. You're going to MISS sometimes. But what separates the greats is the APPROACH. You have to step up and be

FOCUSED when you're taking the last shot or making a much needed play. Your confidence has to be high be- cause you have to be able to come through and COUNTER if things don't go according to plans. The mind is so KEY when it comes to success at anything. Being clutch is being confident in knowing that you are prepared to get it done no matter the CIRCUM- STANCES. You have to create that in your mind and it has to stay there. It can never WAVER.

To me, being clutch is for everyone. I don't believe in CLUTCH as a category. It's just that some players are more prepared for the moment than others. Players have too CONDITION themselves to be ready for any MOMENT at all times. Having a bold confidence and be- ing PREPARED is what allows you to show up in those moments. After I made that shot, I PSYCHED myself out mentally by telling myself, "that's what I do." I believed that, and that's the way I treated those moments every time after. I lived for those moments. I know the feeling you get and the respect that comes with being able to win games. I wanted that respect.

So many college games during the NCAA tournament are won by buzzard beaters and amazing plays. Most kids want to be in those moments and the seed is plant- ed while watching it take place. They see it live, on sports center and on social media. Buzzard beaters are some of the biggest plays in basketball. By normal standards, buzzard beaters are considered clutch. But I want to take it deeper into the mindset and the pressures that come with being cutch.

Clutch is situational. A buzzard beater can be a desperation shot, or a clutch shot. Whats the difference? The difference is the outcome. It's no pressure in making what I call a 50/50 shot. That's the shot that if you miss it, you either win or you go into overtime. It's no risk in that shot. Mentally it's no pressure. You also have bail out shots that are 50/50 shots. Remember basketball mindset is everything. You have to understand the mental game to understand the game. A bail out shot comes from players who will rather take a three when down two, so if they miss, it was a deep shot, and they have a comfort zone if they do miss. Instead concentrating and trying to get to the free throw line or tie the game and go into overtime, they settle for the "50/50." Now the 50/50 can win games, but it's a shot anyone can take and make. It doesn't make you clutch. Now a clutch mentality down two who is confident and want to send a dagger, will step up to take the three to win the game and burry their opponent. You may say how do you know, you know because it's a character trait. There are those who want to take the shot and live and die with the outcome. Those are the guys who are mentally pre- pared for the moment.

Being clutch isn't making game winners, it's rising up and making the crucial shots when needed. It's a pos- session game and an example of that, is if you're in a game going back and forth and you're in the fourth quarter, the opposing team has a five point lead, the

clock is down to one minute and it's a five point game and you're down. Your opponent comes down and miss. You get the ball and get fouled. forty six seconds left. You step up to the line and get two free throw shots. You make both. That's clutch. You made it a one possession game. If you had missed those shots, it's an opportunity that it would become a three point game if they score again. Your opponent comes down and burn the clock, it runs down half way and a player makes a big stop! That's clutch defensively! It's Twenty two seconds left in the game and your'e down three. Two things may happen in this situation. Your coach may call a timeout and go two for one, meaning score quick then foul and hope they miss a free throw or two. Your team get's the ball back for the last possession. Or he may say go for three and the tie and make sure no time is left, that will be the last shot. Now, your thought process in these moments are what makes a player clutch. You can say whatever you want to your teammates, but your mind and heart knows the truth. This is when mentally, you believe that you're going to come through. You have put your self in this situation before all the times you visioned yourself being here taking the last shot. Instead of being nervous or allowing your nerves to get the best of you, you're confident and ready for action. Clutch isn't being perfect, it's giving yourself a confident chance to be successful. And with this mindset. You will make the big ones.

Chapter IX:
High School

THE DAY I walked on a COLLEGE campus, I knew I was ready for this LIFESTYLE. My Mom's and I went on my visit to Georgetown University after being OFFERED a scholarship. When we got to campus, we walked right through the middle of the campus where the dorms and classrooms were. We were on our way to sit down and talk to legendary, hall of fame coach John Thompson. As we walked, I saw the students going to and from classes and just IMAGINED myself going to classes on this cam- pus. It was the first time that I have been to this campus and it's in DC my HOME town. The other students were looking at us and they just knew that this tall African American kid that looks no more than 12 years old, has to be a BALLER. I had a baby face with no facial hair and a fresh temple taper hair cut. I WALKED like a ball play- er so it wasn't difficult to see. My confidence was EXU-BERANT, it showed on me like clothes. I was so excited to be there. I watched Georgetown play and was a fan of Patrick Ewing, Reggie Williams and David Wingate growing up. I loved how they wore the grey tees under their jersey's and the grey high top Skye Force Nike SNEAKERS. I wanted those sneakers and tee shirts so bad. I was a step close to getting them.

The only thing that I knew about COLLEGE basketball was what i saw on TV. I didn't know anything about how you get to college, the REQUIREMENTS or anything until my Senior year of High School. I was a pretty good player, getting recruited by a lot of schools across the COUNTRY. Before this craze of receiving an "offer," we received HAND written interest letters. If you received a hand written letter, that school

WANTED you. I had a letter from every small school in the country. From Di- vision 1 to Division 3 and this was at the beginning of the season after I had a really good summer. The first time I played High School Summer League, was my INTRODUCTION to being a local favorite. It was the SUMMER of my Senior year that i had my first full INTRODUCTION to High School basketball and it was my break out Summer. The Summer League was at Suitland High School in Suitland, MD. We played against all Maryland Schools and at the time, I didn't think Maryland guys could PLAY. Maybe a few of them. I saw Walt Williams who was one of my faves and later on i met Henry Hall another one of my faves. Maryland's FINEST if you ask me. I had traveled everywhere play- ing with my adult team and remembered how we use to dominate all the Maryland courts we played on, so I thought this would be the same.

My very first game, changed that though process. We played against Duval High School and I never heard of that school before. I thought that my high school team was very good. We had a lot of skilled players. Just like my team playing with the older guys, I though this was going to be EASY. Boy was I wrong. My LESSON from this was that regardless of skill sets, when playing a team game, it takes a certain level of teamwork and IQ to be a SUCCESSFUL team. Playing with older players, things happen as you expect them too. Not with younger players. So it was an INTRODUCTION to leadership for me as well.

Duval had two players that I remember the most, Carl Turner and Stacy Robinson Jr. These two guys could FLAT out ball and I would get to find that out really fast. The whole game I felt like i was playing against both of them. Carl would hit a 3, I would score, then Stacy would get a dunk, then I would score, I felt like It was two against 1 and the other 7 players on the floor did not matter. But Duval did have another player that could play, but I don't remember who that was. NEED- LESS to say I scored my 30 points but it wasn't good enough to win. We lost by single digits. The whole game, it felt like we were playing catch up and we never had control. They were having fun and we were CHASING our tails. I felt that something was DIFFERENT. I had to figure it out. And figure it out I did.

I went home to Malcolm X basketball courts, and I told my older guys what had happened. They talked to me about being a LEADER and leading by example. They said it's not like playing with us, because we are all leaders and we know what to EXPECT from each other, but that's not the same as playing with your school teammates. You're the man and you have to do more. Right from that conversation I got better. I gained more KNOWLEDGE. Knowledge is IQ and IQ is key! I understood what they meant because when my neighborhood friends started to get better, i would pick them to run with me against the older guys. I LEAD that team so now it was time for me to lead my summer league team.

The rest of the summer league was ok. We finished with 4 wins and 4 losses and I learned a lot about leadership and MYSELF as a player. It was a summer for GROWTH. The purpose of High School summer league was served. It's about team and player growth. I also realized that I was a SPECIAL player. Every game that i played after the first game against Duval, the stands were packed. Packed with guys from my neighborhood and people I didn't know. I really didn't know they were there to see me at first, I just had fun playing the game and I didn't really pay ATTENTION to what was going on in the stands. Word of mouth had spread around about this skinny kid named Lonnie Harrell.

At the end of the Summer League, they selected players to play in the All Star game. I didn't know anything about it. Some how, my cousins boyfriend (Earnie) had a friend, who's nephew was in the game and he had mentioned that I was supposed to be playing. I was around my way on the outdoor courts playing, when Earnie pulled up and said yo, you supposed to be playing in this All Star game at Suitland, it's about to start in 5 minutes. I asked someone to take my game and I RAN off the court and hopped in the car with him. I had to go home first and tell my Mother, then drive 15 minutes to the game. When we ARRIVED, the game had 5 minutes remaining in the first half. As I walked to the bench, the crowd started getting LOUD, I couldn't hear what they were saying, but it started getting louder and louder. Then I noticed the players turning around looking to see why, and even players on the court were looking to see what was going on. What was going on was ME. People came to see me play! They were excited when I walked in and gave me a big WELCOME. That set the tone for me because I loved to play and I wanted to show people how good I could play. That was my MOTIVATION. It wasn't that i had to prove anything to anybody, I wanted to show everybody what i could do. I was handed a tee shirt which was the uniform, I already had my gear on because I was hooping outside, but to my surprise, Earnie had bought me a fresh pair of sneakers for the game. My favorites, High top Airfare One's. At the time it was my favorite sneaker with the silver strap and stripe. I was FRESH! I always felt that if you LOOK good, you FEEL good, you PLAY good!

I missed the first half, but the Coach started me the 2nd half. As soon as the game began, I went right to work. I scored, dunked, shot deep 3's, made some nice moves, broke some ankles, made some crazy shots, nice passes and FINISHED the game with 27 points in one half and got MVP. This was when I proved WHO I really was as a player from the response I got from my PEERS and the basketball community. I had never played a full High School season, so this was all new to me. I started get- ting letters from Schools after COLLEGE Coaches who attended summer league got to see me play. My life changed after one summer. That was my first experience with college coaches. I knew nothing about that process, and it was more LEVELS to reach in this process.

Now prior to this, the two previous years of high school were BAD for me. Although i come from a single parent household with an AMAZING Mother and older sister, I had a very strong SUPPORT group nearby. I had a very SPIRITUALLY strong family in my neighbored. My Grandmother, Uncle, Aunt and Cousin, all lived together and in the same complex that I live in with my Mom. I saw them everyday. I was the youngest in the family. Everyone finished High School or College, but I wanted to test the waters in the STREETS. It's what i knew, what i was around and most of my friends were out there. My first two years of High School, I wasn't eligible to play. I was SMART, but i made dumb decisions. I PASSED my classes and was able to continue to the next grade by showing up and doing enough to finish what i missed and was able to get decent grades by scoring HIGH on my city test. I tested very well. After that summer, I had people on my back telling me about the OPPORTUNITIES I had to attend college. Remember, I knew nothing about the the College process. I was blessed to had attended Eastern High School and having the best PRINCIPAL ever, Mr. Ralph H Neal. Mr. Neal from the day I met him showed me that he cared about his students and his faculty. Because of that CULTURE he created, getting what I needed for college was avail- able. i just had to do my part. Then everything changed.

My cousin, was a ball player and a street HUSTLER. He played on the Mackin High School team with Johnny Dawkins and was also the VALEDICTORIAN of his class. He had just came home from jail, and showed up on my playground court while I was playing. He sat and watched me play until I was done. Afterwards, I went over to talk to him and he gave me a crazy look then said he heard I was being a knuckle head and not going to school. I asked who told him that and he said it doesn't matter, he know it's TRUE. He said that's the end of that and you're going to school. After that sum- mer day, every morning he was at my house to pick me up and take me to a COURT to play against older guys he knew that could play. This was a new EXPERIENCE for me and a different approach to preparing myself for something greater and development. He had played with other great players like Johnny Dawkins and he knew what it took to get to that level.

One of his good friends was Melvin Middleton. Melvin is a D.C. LEGEND and the first person I left outside of Southeast to hoop with, that wasn't a league. We played streetball. My cousin brought him up to my courts at Malcolm X so I could see him play. After we played there, we went and played at three different courts that same day. Melvin was the BEST point guard I had ever seen or played with at that time. He was so DECEPTIVE with the ball and could get by anyone. He was quick but not fast, and had a Smooth glide as if he was moving in slow motion. The defense would be watching him and forget about defending us because he would go by his man so easy and they had to help or it would be lay up after layup. He passed just as well as he handled the ball. I would get wide open shots and didn't have to do much to get open. Melvin had that street ball SWAGGER back then. The difference was, he was a High School Champion and was the starting Point Guard on the best High School team in the country. His team went 31-0. This was my hooping partner for the summer.

A part of playing ball with Melvin, was my cousin teach- ing me another aspect of the game. He wanted me to learn how to score without the ball. That was one of the things he had learned from Johnny Dawkins. He would tell me stories about Johnny and Johnny was one of his favorite players. He had the opportunenitc to play and watch Johnny become a great player.

I learned a few things playing with Melvin. I learned to be deceptive from and how to MANIPULATE defenders. Watching him taught me these things that i never knew myself. Wherever we went, we had our five. Guys they knew who could COMPETE and just loved to play, but wasn't serious ballers. They were actually street or hood dudes. Melvin would handle the ball and get me in positions to score and I would shoot the MAJORITY of the time. The other players would just DEFEND, re- bound and hustle. I learned so much about scoring play- ing with them. The PRESSURE was on me to deliver, but Melvin really made it easy for me, nobody could guard him. My next task was what I really think played the biggest part in DEVELOPMENT for me. I had all the skills early, it was tough playing with the older guys and a very physical game. But playing in an hostile environment with a different kind of athlete was the icing on the cake. Every Tuesday, we played at the Lorton Reformatory or called the Lorton Correctional Complex. Lorton was one of the most NOTORIOUS prisons in the U.S. It was a place that criminals would ask the judge to not send them there or inmates would ask to be transferred to another prison. I was a teenager and going there every week to play against the INMATES. There were so many talented inmates in prison. We have heard the stories about those who could have had basketball careers if they had not gone to jail. The crazy part about it, I was EXCITED!

The first time we went, I can REMEMBER the experience as if it happened yesterday. When we first pulled up to the prison, we were greeted by correctional officers and we ENTERED through the staffs entrance. After we were searched, they told us we couldn't take anything extra in there. Whatever we were playing in, thats what we had to wear. Afterwards, we walked through a hall that had big windows and doors, and you could see IN- MATES in the recreation yard. This day they were all standing by the doors waiting to get in. Some were allowed to come in and watch us PLAY. Once we got in, the inmates who were playing were shooting around and warming up. I thought we were playing against a FOOTBALL team how strong these guys looked.

The doors opened and the inmates were let in the same HALLWAY we were walking down. They were walking around and PASSING us rushing to get in. My cousin said to me they can't guard you, take the hits and keep going. They're going tor try and intimidate you, but you're good, no worries. I wasn't thinking about fighting anyway. I just wanted to hoop. I LOVE it. I was just watching how they warmed up and tried to pick out who was the BEST player so I can guard him. It was one guy about 6'2, slim dark-skinned and jumped real high on his shot, I wanted to guard him.

I was super competitive. Every time I played, no matter where, playground, rec center, anywhere, I wanted the best player. The game was about to start. We were MATCHING up at the circle, everyone slapped hands and stood by who they were guarding. The correctional officer overseeing the game came to the center of the court and said a few WORDS about sportsmanship be- fore we started. It was game time. You could hear the other inmates on the side talking and calling out bets. It was live in there. I could hear guys from my hood who were incarcerated, calling my name and telling me to show out. They were bragging on me and EXCITED that I was there. It MOTIVATED me and I was ready to perform!

First POSSESSION after jump ball, we got the tip. Whenever I got the ball FIRST, I always catch and take a deep shot from WHEREVER I received the ball. That was my HEAT check (the way to check and see if I'm on to start the game) and to help rid of early BUTTER- FLIES. I use to make the the game happen, I didn't let it happen. When i shot it, the players on the opposing team said, "damn!" This kid crazy. I missed the shot. They got the REBOUND and we got back on defense. They came down and threw the ball in the paint. It was so physical, the two players involved in the play in the post, were banging each other like two football lineman. The shot went up, he missed and I jumped to get the REBOUND. I didn't box out and tried to use my athleticism and just jump high to get the rebound, then POW! I felt a pain in my back that felt like someone hit me with a BAT. I went flying out of bounds into the wall that was about FIVE feet from the court. Although I was in pain, I didn't show it. I knew I couldn't because that would show a sign of WEAKNESS. I played through it and the pain went away after awhile. I didn't know who hit me, but it was a forearm to the back I would find out later in the game. A few plays later, Melvin threw me the ball and said bring him this way. I listened and started to go off a pick he was setting for me, and then BAM, he laid the defender out with the hardest forearm to the chest. It was the guy who had HIT me on the rebound that sent me out of bounds. After the pick, I paused to look at the after math before I took the shot. The DEFENDER got up and said good one. Game on.

The whole game was physical, no dirty plays after my first hit. I guess that was an attempt to put fear in me because I was so young. But it didn't work because I grew up playing with the older guys in my neighborhood and I wasn't allowed to call for fouls. I had to take the hits and keep moving. Even If I complained for a call, i didn't get it. No blood, no foul they would say. This was how I became tough. I played football until I was 14, so I was sought of a late bloomer for organized basketball. So some of the things other players knew, I still didn't know. I git the raw version from players who played the game, but the skipped a lot of the beginning stages of the game.

When it was time for me to go to school and join the team, I grew from 6'2 to 6'6 that summer of my Senior year. I was now focused and ready to handle business. The hooking school and playing around with my grades was over with. It was time to do it for real. The team from the summer was a little different now. We added a few young players that were really talented. From my experience over the summer, I knew this was my opportunity to lead. I had so many classes, teachers and experiences over the summer that made me a knew player and ready for anything.

Before the season started, the big thing was intramural basketball league. I can honestly say there were players that were good enough to play on the school team, but they wanted to hustle and hang in the streets. The games were so good and competitive, everybody in the School would be in the gym to watch the games. That's were I made my name and became the leader of the team. Those games were fun and allowed me to play freely and show my teammates, the coaches who were there watching and the students what I could do.

When practice began, I was focused and payed pay attention to everything and every detail. I wanted to learn all about the game. I didn't play in middle school and the first two years I didn't do what I was supposed to and wasn't eligible. I didn't play AAU because I didn't know anything about it until the summer before my senior year for Executive III. When I saw all the guys on the team, I didn't want to play with them. It was all the best players in the area. Those same guys made up most of the All Metropolitan Team that year. I didn't know any- thing about it, but I played ball everyday all day, and I think that's what was best for me.

The season started and immediately i made a name for my self by playing at a high level and very efficient. People started coming to our games and the Stands would fill up. The game was easy because of my experiences and playing with older guys. But the piece that was added to my game that I didn't know I needed were the fundamentals. We had an older Coach by the name of Mr. NeSmith who was the assistant coach. He was old school and use to stay on me about the fundamentals. I really didn't think he liked me, because he stayed on me and I felt that I could never make him happy. In practice, no matter what I did to make the others get excited, a play or a move I did, he would look at me with a mean mug on his face and wouldn't crack a smile. He would yell at me if he felt like it I would say, because I didn't remember doing anything wrong. It wasn't later until I figured out that I was his example. Our team was young and we had a lot to learn, I was a senior and the best player, so he would yell and scream at me so the other players would know that If i can get yelled at and take it, they can too. He knew I could take it and that was his reason. It all helped and made me a better player.

We had a lot of good players that year. Every school was competitive, regardless of the record. You had a team ready to compete and a High School superstar on each team. I was up for that every game. I didn't take a lot of shots, I had a bunch of young guns that shot more than me. I played to win and didn't concentrate on scoring alone. From playing on the playground in my hood and having to play to win and stay on or go home, i learned how to do whatever it's needed to win. I lead our team in scoring, but i was unselfish, played defense, rebound, hustle, assisted and made plays. I was only taking 15 shots a game and I averaged twenty+ points per game shooting close to 65% a game from the field. I didn't miss a lot in high school. I couldn't because my young team- mates didn't pass the ball.

When things rose to another level for me, was when we played the number one team in the country at our gym. I don't know how this game got scheduled, but it happened, on my floor, at my school where I was the man! I knew the crowd would be huge, but it was sold out for the girls game before our game. Then I noticed something different. All these men were in there with college team jackets on. Black and white guys. My coach took me in his office and said, look, it's a lot of college coaches out there to see these guys you are about to play against. I'm going to put the ball in you hands so they can see you. Don't try and do too much and make your- self look stupid, just play your game. I felt nervous after he said that for the first time. At first I was hyped and ready to go, but after the talk, my stomach started turn- ing and I was nervous. My teammates thought I was focused because I was quiet, but I went blank. I didn't have any thoughts or any questions in my mind. I was just blank and my stomach felt weird.

My Moms use to come to all of my football games, and has never been to one of my basketball games. It was the middle of the season and she came walking through the door. It was so many people outside that couldn't get in, but one of my teammates saw her and got her in. When I saw her, i relaxed. I was still empty of any thoughts, my stomach wasn't as bad, but I still felt weird. It was time for the game to start. I had on my new Adidas Forums the North Carolina blue high tops with the strap and white stripes. My favorite sneakers of all time. We warmed up and lined up at the circle for jump ball. Beside me was the best defender in the country and he said I got him and pointed his finger in my face as if I wasn't standing there. My face got hot and my body started burning like the sun came in the gym. I was heated and angry! Game on.

This day everything I did worked. I don't remember missing a shot, I really don't remember much about the game except we lost by 20 points. but after the game, you would have thought we won. My friends and fans and students at the school ran on the floor and was

jumping on me and pulling me and started saying you're going to College. I'm lost and still kind of out of it, then one of the girls on the basketball team that kept the stat book and brought it to me and said, you had a triple double. Then when i looked, fifty five was circled. Me not knowing, said we had more points than fifty five. She said no Lonnie, you had fifty five points. My most dropped. I had never scored that many points ever and I didn't try to. I didn't have a mindset to score that many points, i just had the mindset to win. I was in a zone and was doing my best to help us win the game, and this game scoring was needed. The guy that was guarding me who was the best defender in the country, had just gave up fifty five points in front of college coaches. He mad me look great! The only memory i had from this game was an illegal dunk. A shot had went up and I crashed the boards and took off. The ball had went over my head, so I grabbed the rim for support, because I collided in the air with their center who was seven feet tall. Once i grabbed the rim to protect myself for landing, I looked back, the ball was in reach. I grabbed the ball with the hand that wasn't holding the rim, and dunked the ball back in. I knew that was illegal, but it happened so quick without a thought, I did it anyway. The crowd went crazy and the whistle blew. I landed and was laughing jogging back to defense, to only find out that they called a foul. I was telling on myself because I grabbed the rim. It happened so fast, the ref didn't see it. It happened for me in slow motion. The crowd went crazy and some were on the floor because the game was so crowded and it wasn't any seats left. But I was play- ing out of my mind.

After the game against the top team in the Nation, for next few games, the assistant coach from Georgetown was in attendance watch me. We didn't know why he was there for sure because there was no communication between us. The buzz around the school was that he was there to see me. Then the next game, the head coach of Georgetown came to the game. The word on the street was he didn't come out to see many players play. By him being at that game, he really was interested in a player on one of those teams.. Turns out the player was me.

Chapter X:
College Part I "Hoya Saxa"

My Moms and I arrived at the gym on Georgetowns campus. It was my Mom's first time there. I had been there before for the Eddie Saah Summer League. The doors stay closed and it's paper over the windows, and tape covering any cracks to prohibit anyone from peek- ing in the gym. Coach Thompson ran closed practices and did not want anyone to see what was going on. What goes on in the gym, stays in the gym. The gym, McDonough arena, had pics of all the players who attended the school on the wall behind the basket, closest to the office stairs, that went on to the NBA. We walked across the gym, passed the pictures and up the stairs that lead to the basketball office. Once we got to the office, there were trophies and the old Georgetown High top Nikes I loved that Patrick Ewing use to wear. I was a huge Patrick Ewing fan, I mean who wasn't in D.C. at the time. Patrick Ewing was our basketball hero. We loved the team sneaks and his short sleeved shirts that had a small pic of the sneakers on one shoulder. That was the Georgetown look.

One thing that stood out in the office, was a flat basketball on Coach (John Thompson Jr.) desk. Coach wasn't in the office yet, but the teams academic advisor was there. Her name was Mary Fenlon. We talked a little about the school and it's academics before coach came in. Pretty much she wanted to know where my grades stood at the time. This was my focus year and I was serious about my School work. My Principal, counselors and teachers at Eastern Sr. High school were the best. They stayed on me and pushed me to qualify for college. I had my grades in order and I got my SAT scores before the season started during my Junior year. Our High School coach made everyone take it Junior year, to get a feel for it, and we could take it multiple times if needed. I didn't need to take it again, my scores could get me into any School that I wanted to attend after the first time that I had taken the test.

Coach came in the office and I didn't realize he was that big and tall until I was close up to him. He was a giant. Coach as we called him, or Coach Thompson, when speaking to outsiders, or "Big John" we called him amongst each other. He sat down and we got right to it. I asked why did he have a deflated basketball on his desk and he told me that it's a reminder and a symbol. It re- minded him that the ball will lose its air one day and that's why education is so important. What are you go- ing to do when the ball doesn't bounce anymore. Quickly I learned my first lesson. We dream of being superstar athletes, but where I am from, nobody thought any of us would make it, nor did we doubt that we could, but no one told me how or the end game and what life would be like if I didn't. I did get to see what that could possibly be like because I saw it everyday growing up in the hood. I didn't see success as the world portrayed it. But the success I did know about was survival.

That meeting was the most informative meeting or discussion that I have had about college after that day. I learned how the NCAA system works, I learned about the Coach and why he wanted me at the university. He told me how important it was to graduate. After my tour of the campus and meeting the professors and priest, we returned back to the gym to coaches offices. The meet- ing ended with Coach offering me a scholarship and asked me to commit that day. Before I could respond, he told me to take the scholarship now, or he would give it to someone else that wanted it. My Moms didn't like that as an offer, but more so a threat. She politely spoke up for me and said, thank you but no thank you. We will not accept it at this time. Like my Moms, I didn't like how it was presented, so we got up and walked out.

Coach attended my next game and kept the communication going. I eventually signed with Georgetown University. Since I lived in D.C. where the University was located, it was a big deal! My life changed immediately. When the news reported it, I became a local celebrity and home town hero over night. To play for Georgetown was every DC kids dream.

One of the perks of going to a local school was gym access. I would go up to the gym and workout and play with the other returning players and Alumni. My first time going up to workout, I worked out with the coaches son. We were shooting shots from each spot on the court. It was my first time working out there or even with someone I didn't know and it was just awkward to me. Empty gym and shooting with a stranger. He shot first and he was a really good shooter. He was a Junior and would be a Senior the next season when I arrived. After he shot, It was my turn. I made a few shots then started to miss some. Streaky set, but he started talking and saying, "They told me you could shoot. That was a lie." So immediately I saw where this was going. I didn't respond and then started making shots. He started throwing my passes harder and I continued to make more shots. It's just the competitor in me. Any little thing I would use as motivation. The other players were in the weight room working out and then they started slowly coming to the court to get up shots. Later that evening, when we had enough players, we played five on five. This is what I was waiting for.

Whenever you go to a new team, a new School or joining a team as a freshman or a rookie, you always have a point to prove to yourself. Nobody else, to yourself. You have to know and feel that you belong. If you don't feel this way, then you don't want to be the best. Having butterflies, being nervous and wanting the best for yourself is all natural. You just can't let those things control you. You have to control them. Preparing yourself and working smart, doing the things that's going to benefit you as a player, will help you control and conquer your emotions and fears. Mastering your game will give you the confidence to compete at any level. Follow the mental game up with the physical preparation and you will be fine. But, always strive to be better than just fine. Strive to be great.

The first game was played by the older players. I had to sit on the side and watch before I could play. Even after the game, you don't get to pick a team. The upperclass- men picks the team for you. You just have to hope they pick you up. Watching them play and how high their energy level was, was amazing! It was very Physical and high intense defense. High school players didn't play like this. These guys were so much stronger and faster. When I got on the floor, I ran as fast as I could and played as if it was a real game. That's how much I had to put out to keep up. The first game I passed a lot and it hid that I was trying to keep up with the pace. The next game I was more involved and my shot was on. I didn't do a lot of dribbling because I wasn't in the same shape as they were in, so I saved my energy as much as I could. I saved my energy so that I could shoot. Catch and shoot was my only focus, and I shot the ball great. I was playing against the Senior that I had shot around with BEFORE the games had begun, and It was my time to show him how good I can shoot. After making the comment about "they told me you could shoot. That was a lie," I got my energy from the adrenaline of being competitive. I wasn't tired anymore and started making every shot. I heard the players saying "don't let him catch it," and "sh*t" whenever I caught a pass and had a good look. I set the tone and jumped past him immediately! I showed him that I could shoot just as well as he could, but I could shoot all kinds of ways. I was able to shoot on the move, in transition, off screens and off the dribble.

Needless to say that I made my first mark before the season started. This challenge would continue once the school year begun. We had a workout schedule and we would play pickup when we returned to school before the season started. I worked out all summer at the school and played in the local summer leagues and was ready to get on campus and show my progress. Some of the players returned home after they completed sum- mer School. It was very few of us there for about two months. Once everyone returned, it was some of the most intense and competitive games ever. Everyone was going at each other and putting egos in check. Again I was playing against the Senior (Coaches son), but this time I was stronger and ready. Everyone was back at the School including All American, Alonzo Mourning. We were on teams and we were killing everybody. One game, I was playing against Coach son and I was having my way and scoring all kinds of ways. Alonzo said to coach son, "you're letting a freshman bust your a**." After Zo said that, he started getting more physical, fouling, throwing elbows and just showing his frustration.

THE GAME WAS very physical and not a lot of calls for fouls being made. Then one possession, I was on defense, he drove to the basket, I stripped the ball and fouled him on contact. As I was turning to run down court, he turned and punched me in the face. I paused after I'd got hit, and he threw his guards up and started bouncing on his toes. It looked funny to me and I laughed then my teammates grabbed me. After that, the players grabbed him as well and Coach and his advisor stood at the top of the balcony that overseas the court and that ended the whole situation. It's cameras every- where so they were watching us play and ran out after he threw the punch. But me as a freshman and getting hit by a senior didn't intimidate me at all. It made me want to go even harder. I grew up fighting with my friends everyday. Him hitting me didn't phase me at all, because honestly in my mind, I figured he didn't know any better and the punch didn't effect me. But because of principal, I was going to get him back. But that never happened. I was over It by the time I left the gym. I got called to the office to talk to the advisor. The first thing she said was, "please don't let anything happen to him. He's a good person and he was just upset. Please don't get any of your friends to hurt him." I know she saw my face as I got angry. But I wasn't angry for long. One thing about growing up in a God fearing home, is that you learn to reason and think about consequences. Her statement rubbed me the wrong way and it really made me think about why I was here. If she thought of me as a hoodlum, why even ask me to come to your school and play for your program? I then had to look at the greater picture and understand that she was a part of their family and he had wronged me without thinking about his consequences and she did. Because of her comments, it let me know that retaliation wasn't necessary and that I now knew what I was up against. They showed their hand. I had no fear of them or anyone on that campus. Only thing I cared about was surviving the streets of D.C.

Adversity will either make or break you. You have to be able to deal with anything that gets in your path and over come it. Games aren't the only part of winning. You have to win small goals and challenges daily. It will al- ways be something that gets in the way to take your focus, but you have to remember your goals and focus on that. I loved basketball more than anyone, and I wasn't going to let anything stop me from that. Being young and your first time away from home, and having real responsibilities, you have to check yourself and grow up fast. One of the biggest developments trades of the best athletes, is MATURITY. Maturity is the quick mental developer. When you see a young player who has good fundamentals, understands and use mid-range, or plays with a poise unlike other kids, I would bet that that kid is more mature than the other players. Maturity is also that thing that allows mental development and a better understanding of the game.

My Freshman season I bought in to my role and played my part the best that I could. My coach wasn't to fond of my style of play. He called me, "Boogaloo" because he said that I had a lot of showboat in my game. He limited my game and I was used as a passer and a catch and shoot player. I felt caged in and it was kind of difficult trying to figure it out, but it was a part of the process of my maturation. I didn't know that then, but it all worked out for me towards the end of the season. It also helped my game later on in my career. All of these experiences whether good or bad, had to happen to create the player that I have become. All the trials and adversity prepared me for the next level of challenges. Some say I picked the wrong school for my style of play and that I was ahead of my time. That may have been true, but that stop was necessary in my development as a man.

When the season started and it was time to play the real games, I was used in a very limited role. Didn't play a lot of minutes, but i was used in crucial moments of games. I was used to inbounds on key possessions, against the press, or if we needed points late in games, he would call my number. That gave me hope as a freshman. I remember playing in key moments against Syracuse, St. Johns, Seton Hall and even UConn when the Big East was the best conference in the country. In these games I made big plays and made some big shots. But the biggest takeaway, was how he groomed as and sped up that maturation process and showed us how to be men.

Freshman year was a lot of fun, although playing limited minutes, but it was only the beginning. I didn't have any worries. Three more years to go, we had six upperclassmen and six freshman. We also had the BIG EAST player of the year and All American on our team, Alonzo mourning. I just wanted to learn as much as I could and keep adding to my game. Watching the player of the year showed me the work ethic it took to get to the next level and having the benefit of working with the former players who were now in the NBA helped as well. It was always something and someone to learn from. Practices were so intense and a lot of running. After awhile, you get use to the running. You get use to it because you understand that it's to help your conditioning and not punishment. You push yourself to get in the best shape possible. Thats a part of MATURITY, looking at the work to better you as a player. But there are sometimes when the running is punishment. When you have six fresh- man on a team, it's definitely going to be times when the punishment is warranted. A bunch of young kids away from home for the first time and a lot of freedom, is an appetite for destruction. We were just young and having fun. There were times when our fun would bring about discipline and have the whole team running, even after games.

Having the best player in our league at the time, made it easy for some of us. Every team you're playing against focus on the top player.

The scouting report focused on stopping him. That made a way for the rest of us to do our jobs and our jobs only without any pressure. All the pressure was on him. My job was to relieve some of that pressure and I had the tools to help do that. I was a really good passer and that is what got me some minutes. When teams played zones, as most did, he would post up with two players guarding him, and coach wanted us to get him the ball by any means. Yep get him the ball while he's being double teamed. He was that good. In practice, sometimes I would work with him on different ways to get him the ball. Coach would have us working on all kinds of entry passes and lobs. One of the passes I re- membered working on that we did only twice in the same game, was against Miami in a home game. Most of the time when he would post up on the low block, they would front him. It would be one defender in the front and one behind him. It would also be a defender on the ball and they would leave the furthest pass open on the opposite side, which would take a skip pass to get there and give the defense enough time to rotate with good on ball pressure. I would be at the top of the key while the ball was on the wing when we would attempt this pass. He would point to me signaling the wing player to swing the ball to me, he would reverse pivot and pin the man behind him, so that he would get the position under the basket as if to be boxing out, and I would throw a pass off the low corner of the back board and it would drop in his hand and he would catch it and finish. The ball would hit the back board and the defense wouldn't see that coming. It worked a few times and then we wouldn't do it again. It was get him the ball however, even if I had to sacrifice the pass as a missed shot.

One of the benefits of playing this style (inside out), when you pass it to a dominant post player in the paint, if he doesn't have the shot, he would kick it back out for you to shoot it. I had the green light to shoot it when he passed it out, and that is one of the highest percentage shots in the game. He was unselfish and didn't force many shots, so we would get those looks often.

Playing your role has to be done with a positive mind set. There are always going to be times when we think we deserve better or more, but we have to do our part to make it happen. Nothing is never given and always earned. We have to work towards our goals and set our minds on the journey. The journey is the process and where we spend majority of our time in search of the tools we need to obtain and reach our goals. It's those things where the foundation and the humbling is rooted. During this process, who we would become as a player was being created. Our characters were being polished and it's probably that part of success that get's over looked at the end. The grind doesn't get glorified or rewarded. Only how you finish earns trophies. But the greatest reward is when you look back at the road traveled and all the people and the things that were apart of making it happen. I learned so much that season, and was looking forward to the next Chapter, Sophomore year! This was going to be a big year for me. I was willing to do whatever it took to prepare and get ready for it! Towards the end of Freshman year, we made it to the NCAA Tournament and I was a starter. The first game we played against South Florida, I had a great game. It was a statement game for me and I definitely made one. This mentally catapulted me ahead for my next season.

The summer entering my sophomore year was really big for my confidence. DC basketball summers were mine. I was a big draw in Summer Leagues around the city and even traveled to other cities to play and learn from other players. At Georgetown University, we had a summer league called the "Kenner League." The Kenner League was a NCAA sanctioned summer league for college players in the D.C., Maryland and Virginia areas. That summer, I let it be known that I was ready to hit the college scene different from my freshman year. I was a better player from all the things that I've learned the year be- fore, and I was physically ready. My mind, my condition- ing and skills, were ready!

During the Kenner League games, the Georgetown Freshman all had to play on a team together called "The Tombs." The team was sponsored by The Tombs, a sports bar in Georgetown, that was frequented by students from the University. Our sophomore year, we were placed on different teams. This was the beginning of my breakout. I had already put the city on notice of my performances in other summer leagues, so now I had to notify the students, fans and coaches of Georgetown about my game. That summer, I was one of the best players in the league.

Georgetown had just committed two incoming Fresh- men that were McDonalds All Americans and an International player. One of them was a Center and the other was forward/wing and the international player was a Point Guard. I felt no threat over the excitement about the incoming Freshman. I was actually excited because Alonzo had moved on to the NBA and we had two players 6'9 and 6'11 coming in. We had Don Reid re- turning who was one of my favorite teammates at the time because of his work ethic and how physical he played the game. Don was an enforcer and looked out for his teammates on the court. If he had to set an extra hard pick, or give a hard foul to an opposing player, for taking a cheap shot on one of his teammates, he would. He was one of the strongest and most athletic big men in college basketball. So adding the two freshman bigs had good promise.

When we started preseason workouts, our trainer, Ms. Lorie Michaels, who was one of my faves, was really good at getting us prepared for the season. Our fitness test consisted of timed runs. Outdoors we had to try and run a 4 minute mile, I had the third best time on the team clocking in a little over four minutes. The other test was indoor sprints on the court. I was in great shape and Ms. Michaels had even told coach that I came in in great shape and looked good. This was my time. I set the tone in practice and after finishing the season starting in the final two NCAA tournament games as a freshman, I came back with a mindset of earning that starting spot as a sophomore. That preseason, I had some outstanding games. But my plans didn't matter.

Chapter XI:

College Part II

The summer after my freshman year was one of my biggest summers at that time. I understood the process and what it was going to take for me to get where I wanted to be. My sophomore season I was more focused and worked harder than the summer of my freshman campaign. It didn't matter to me what everyone else was doing, I was on a high and ready to do my thing.

As soon as Alonzo left to go to the NBA, Georgetown bought in two McDonalds All Americans, Dwayne Spencer a tall 6'11 forward/wing from Louisiana that was similar to me. He could handle the ball and shoot. The other was 6'9 Center Othella Harrington from Mississippi. Othella was young and had a lot of potential. He was expected to fill Alonzo shoes, but those shoes were too big to fill. That season, I was a sophomore and hungry for the season to start. Living in DC, where George- town is located, I stayed on campus and attended summer School and worked out the whole summer. Even when my teammates took their breaks to go home, I stayed and worked out and was in the best shape I had ever been in. I played everyday and worked out with ormer NBA player and Georgetown Alumnus Bay Bay Duren and Pat Ewing. That summer I played every- where. I would go to the gym on campus and play with the pros that would come to the school to play. Then I would go to my neighborhood Congress Park during the week and play pickup in the blazing heat. Show up at all the rec centers with my hoop partners and best friends. Play in leagues and then play at the Kenner League and the Urban Coalition on the weekends. I had a serious Jones! I even played on campus with the students at Georgetown in the community gym.

When pre-season started, the Coaches and the trainers noticed the difference in my work ethic and in my game. I had learned so much playing with the pros and pre- paring for the season that I understood what coach was saying about my flash. I was able to play without the tricks and just get straight to work. Watching Pat Ewing workout with Bay Bay Duren, I learned how to keep things simple. Bay Bay was very close to Coach Thompson and he knew what Coach wanted from me. So he would show me things and help me simplify my game. I use to think basketball was easy already, but after listening and learning from Bay Bay and Pat, the game be- came easier and the physical aspect was the piece that I had to add, and I began working on that when I arrived on campus. My workouts would be all about picking spots that I know I could score from, getting to them and scoring from those spots. He taught me about my fingers and ball control when I dribbled. Mastering "layups." Yes, a simple layup deserved time. It was the most simple things that were my focus the whole summer. Those things translated to the game. That's the game, master- ing the fundamental ASPECTS of the game. When pre- season began, it was time to put all I learned that sum- mer together.

We would always start the season off playing against HBCU's. The big University's pay the smaller schools to play because those games use to be guaranteed wins, so in exchange for messing up the smaller schools records, they would pay them for the guaranteed early win. Coach liked to play the HBCU's because it was putting the money back into black institutions where other black coaches were and some were his friends. The be- ginning of the pre-season, all of the talk was about the new Freshman All Americans. My close friend John Jaques and myself, both had good NCAA tournament showings to end our freshman campaigns, and we were back to earn a continuation and earn our spots. I had earned my starting position in pre-season and I came out the gates full steam ahead! All the work I put in over the summer was paying off. After the first three games, the hype was getting louder and louder. I had my own fan section at the games who called themselves, "LONNIE'S LOONIES." I will never forget them. It was about 30 students that would sit right behind the basket at the Capital Center (our home arena), in the student section and wore shorts with long socks. Long socks was a DC thing at the time and I represented the style at Georgetown.

A lot of the attention was surrounding me early in the season from the students. Then one day at breakfast on campus, I found out that the media was paying attention as well. We were sitting at the table talking and enjoying our free time, and I was handed a news paper by one of my friends. It had my picture on the front of the sports section with the caption, "LONNIE AND THE MIRACLE'S?" The caption was a reference to Reggie Williams and his team after Patrick Ewing had left, they were called "Reggie and the Miracles." The writer was com- paring our team to the time when Reggie Williams lead his team. The buzz was so crazy that it was even rumors of me going HARDSHIP after the season and the season hadn't really started yet. I heard the noise and I was all for it! I just wanted to play and show the world what i could do. I even had a guy contact me and he started coming on campus, he would rent cars for me so I could take my friends to Kings Dominion and get to and from home when I wanted to leave the campus. He would take me to dinner often and make sure I had anything I needed. Not that I needed anything from him because I had my guys and cousins from my hood taking care of me and making sure I had money in my pockets at all times. This guy was working for an agent.

Then I had a big scare at a practice. I was having a in practice battle with a walk on and we know how hard walk ons go.They're trying to earn their keep and earn a scholarship, so they play extra hard. I drove to the bas- ket and he fouled me really hard. I tripped and he pushed me down and I came down on my knee. It was a sharp pain that hurt really bad but I down played the feeling and got up because I was scared it would effect all that I have been working for, and didn't want that to get in my way. The pain didn't last long and I got up and continued on playing. I was fine, at least I thought I was. The next practice I was running and my knee locked. I couldn't straighten my knee out and I was scared. I stopped and wiggled my knees in a circular motion, and my knee unlocked. I didn't tell anybody I just kept going. We had a game the next day and I wanted to play so I kept it to myself. The game before this, I had 17 points at halftime and didn't play in the second half.

The next game day, I had a good warm up, I felt great and I started the game off strong. Still pre-season, we were just getting started and I had 14 early points in the first half. I ran the floor finishing layups, making mid- range shots by catch and shoot and "stealing" points. Stealing points was considered creating the easiest shots possible by cutting and moving and making the uncomfortable shots that I usually would miss. Those were some of the things I was taught over the summer working with Bay Bay. If you can get to your spots and make the shots you know you can make, then that's half the battle.

"Keep the game simple. You're good enough to get yours playing a simple game." - John Bay Bay Duren

I will never forgot those words. Adding that to the skills I already had, I felt like the best player in the gym and it was all from mental things I was taught that I didn't know about the game. After my last bucket scored, I was running back on defense and then CLICK! My knee had locked again. This Time I couldn't hide it. The other times it would go right back to normal after a few circular wiggles. I would shake my leg or motion my knee in a circle and it would go back. This time it didn't and our trainer saw that something wasn't right and I ran off the court and called a timeout in the middle of the play. I was so upset because everything was going well and the start to my season was going well. It's no way that this would be happening to me right now. I was hurting inside. My knee didn't have any pain, but I couldn't STRAIGHTEN it out.

It's over I was thinking. All this hard work to PREPARE for this moment came to an end during Pre-Season of my Sophomore year.

Our trainer, Ms. Michaels checked my knee out and because it happened randomly, she knew that something wasn't right and scheduled an MRI. I was busted! I could no longer hide it and had to see what was wrong. It was clearly something that wasn't going away. After i took the MRI which was one of the WORST experiences of my life, sitting in that tube listening to it knock for an hour, I couldn't move nor could I sleep because I was paranoid and so many things going through my mind. My fear of this injury heightened my CONCERN. I hadn't ever heard of an acl tear or anything like that. When someone hurt their knee, we would just say they BUSTED their knee. The next day I was in class, and I was pulled out by our trainer. She had gotten the results from the MRI. They were positive and I had a floating bone chip in my knee and it would occasionally find its way to the joint in my knee and rest in-between it and CAUSE it to jam. So I thought that I would just have to play with the FLOATING bone chip and I was cool with that as long as I could play and It could go away one day. But that wasn't the case. She told me that I had to have surgery immediately. The chip could find its way in be- tween a joint, tendon and cause more damage. Here I am having the greatest start to my college career and it came crashing down with a knee INJURY.

After I got the news, before I returned to class, I called my mom from a PAYPHONE in the hallway. I told her the news and I CRIED on the phone in the hallway. Everyone was in class at the time, so no one saw me in the hall crying. My mom and her strong FAITH told me that everything would be fine and not to worry that I would come out of this even stronger. After class I was right back in the DOCTORS office getting an exam and prepping for my SURGERY. My surgery was the very next day. They move pretty fast at major colleges. Our trainer was probably the best TRAINER that i had ever had in my career and she was always on the job. While I was getting treatment, in her office, the training room, she had read that Latrell Sprewell's had just had a MICROSCOPIC surgery and returned to play for the Knicks in 12 days. It was an in and out procedure that I had never heard of or knew anything about. She said the good thing is that you have been working on your body and we can control the swelling after your surgery and if you are willing to work HARD and through this, we can beat Sprewell's and have you back in NINE days! I was so excited to hear that because I thought that get- ting surgery was going to have me sitting out for the WHOLE season.

I got the surgery and the same day, I was back in her training room getting cold compression on both of my legs. The rehabilitation has started and we were on a mission to beat Sprewell's nine days. Everyday I would have REHAB that would consist of ultra sound, cold compression, balancing balls, leg weights, upper body bike cardio, footwork drills and the cold world pool. The amount of swelling that I had, i didn't see a NINE day return, but i kept the faith and I kept pushing. Then on the ninth day I was back on the practice floor. We did it. We beat Sprewell's TWELVE day return.

It was the first week of November and my cousin had just called me and asked me what kind of car do I want for my BIRTHDAY. He said "nothing fancy because Coach don't play that and you can't be driving fancy cars on campus, I don't want to get you in trouble." I asked for a minivan so I can drive my friends around. This was on a Wednesday after practice. We had another pre-season game against the Army on Campus the Fri- day coming and he said he'll be at the game and I will get your van this weekend. When Friday hit, I was so excited to be back playing and I didn't miss a beat. I started the game and picked up where I left off. My cousin was sitting court side directly across from our bench and he was so excited about the way i was playing. I had twenty two points at half time. The second half, I didn't start and the third quarter went by and I didn't get back in the game. I looked over at my cousin, and he got up and swung his hand in disgust and put his fist up to the side of his face and said call me and walked out. I didn't get back in the game. I wasn't worried because it was our last pre-season game and the real show was about to be- gin. I scored my points, just making shots, running the floor and finishing. Nothing special, just simple basket- ball.

When we got back to the dorms, myself and my team- mate who was also a sophomore, from Chicago Derek Patterson, played cards in our friends room who played on the Woman's basketball team. I paged (messaged his beeper) my cousin to see what he had to say after the game and to really find out what time I was getting my van, and he didn't respond. I waited awhile and paged him again and he didn't respond. We kept playing cards all night and when we were done, i paged him again be- fore I went to sleep. Still no response. The next morning I got to sleep in because we didn't have practice and it was also the weekend. My phone rang and woke me up. One of my friends called and asked me did my cousin get killed. I quickly responded no, and told him he was at my game the day before. He told me that's what he heard and that he was going to find out. Then i got an- other call and it was from his brother. He told me the news. I dropped my phone in disbelief and couldn't pick it up. He told me that he got killed standing at the phone booth making a call. He always call me right back when I page him, and the call he was making was to me. I was the last one to page him and the last time I saw him he was leaving my game upset because my coach didn't put me back in the game. I was broken. I use to think it was my fault. If I had not paged him at that time, he wouldn't have went to that phone booth to make that call. But this would become a part of my drive. I was angry and upset.

The next few days of practice weren't the same. I was getting calls and nobody would say anything on the other end and then i got a threatening call from someone telling me not to go to the funeral. The next call that came was a shock to me and I could never figure it out. Coach called me to the gym and said that he has friends on the police force and word on the street was that something was supposed to go down at his service. He requested that I didn't attend. I listened and didn't go to the service, but nothing happened. I attended the Funeral and was a pallbearer and I couldn't say no to that. It was a very rough time in my life because the guy who helped prepare me for this level, had been taken away from me. I talked to him before every game and he would hype me up and get my head ready to play. He never missed that call and he knew the time and why i was calling. I missed those calls. I needed those calls. That was my the one person who could keep me level headed and motivated. His support and his knowledge of what this process was all about, I needed. I didn't have a clue! He helped me understand Coach, because I couldn't make reason on my own.

The season was now here. Our first regular season was a home game at the Capital Center. "Lonnie's Loonies" were in attendance. I had a great warmup, went through the routines with the team and now it was time to put the real work in. I was ready to show the world who I was! I sat down with the starting five and they were calling the other teams starters and before they got to us, I got a tap on the shoulder from one of the assistant coaches. He signaled to me to stand up and I got up to see what he wanted, and he said stand right here. After I got up, one of my teammates sat down. I was pulled from the starting lineup after starting in pre-season without being told at the start of the game that I wasn't going to start. To add injury to insult, I didn't get in the game until the the last two minutes to inbound the ball. We had the lead and the team was pressing us. They used me to inbound the ball. I was crushed. I didn't know why, it was a surprise and now I was fighting against my own mind and my emotions. During this time, you couldn't question a coach about their deci- sions, especially a coach such as ours. He was the coaches coach. Dean Smith, Coach K and other coaches use to come and sit in on our practices. How could I question him? This would go on for the whole season. I only played when i was needed.

One game I remember in particular was against UCONN at UCONN. I had been on the bench the whole game and we were losing by twenty points. Late in the game, Coach emptied the bench and put myself and my best friend John on the floor late in the third quarter. This game changed my career and eased my mind about my feelings and my time at Georgetown. UCONN had an All American and four players who would turn out to be NBA players. We entered the game and started a come-back from down twenty points. With nothing to lose and already being thrown in to just finish the game out, John looked at me and said, "let's go to work." Former NBA player Gilbert Arenas once asked, "What's more dangerous? A pit bull in a room of people on a leash or one running free with no leash?" We were running free.

We had nothing to lose. The towel was thrown in, and everyone was just waiting for the time to run out to end the game. It was enough time to win, but the starters and guys who played the most, had an off day. They were playing really bad. We were having a subpar sea- son and our only hope to make it to the NCAA Tournament, would be to win the Big East Tournament. We were Big East Champs the season before, but this season was a challenge because we lost our best player to the NBA and everybody had to step up. This game against UCONN, it was no way we were expected to come back, but we did. We did what we needed to do to win the game. People couldn't believe it. During that run of about ten minutes, I hit three three pointers and finished with sixteen points, five rebounds, three assist and three steals. John had twelve points. between the two of us, we scored twenty eight points in the second half. It was the biggest comeback that season. To close the game out, I got a huge rebound and threw it ahead to a teammate for an easy layup, then turn around and got a steal and a layup myself and the game was over.

After the game, I was sitting in my locker with mixed emotions about what just happened. That was a big game for our season. All season long I wanted to play, i felt that I deserved to play. I practiced hard, I listened, I didn't get in any trouble, and I knew i could compete.

I wanted to play! I had so many questions that i needed answers to and nobody to call. My cousin was gone and I didn't know who else I could talk to to answer my questions. One thing for sure, I never questioned myself. That's how i stayed ready. Doubt can kill your drive, confidence and motivation. Thats why mental toughness is key. As I sat thinking about the game that just ended, a group of media guys surrounded my locker. They were asking questions about the game how I felt and how did we pull this game out and get the win. Then the one question that came and put a halt to the whole inter- view, and answered my questions in my head, was from a young man that wrote for the Washington Post. He looked at me and said, "Lonnie, it seems that you could easily average 20 points in the Big East, why aren't you playing more?" I will never forget that question. Before I could form my lips to answer, it was an assistant coach standing to the side behind the media and as soon as the writer finished asking that question, the assistant coach stepped in and said, "excuse me, can i borrow him for a second?" That was the end of the interview. What happened after that would be the end of Lonnie at G-Town as I was known.

I felt back sided, I lost trust and I didn't understand more than anything why this would happen. I gave my all to the game and to my team. But the words that were said to me when I was pulled away from that press conference, was like a stab to my heart. I lost something that day. When i returned to my seat, that same writer could see something was bothering me, and he said, don't worry about it, I already know what it is. I won't repeat the question. Then another columnist repeated it. Looking over to my left, now it's two coaches standing there watching and listening, I responded with, "I rather not say anything." That comment upset my coaches be- cause I didn't repeat what I was told to say. So as a punishment to that, when we returned back to DC from Connecticut, we arrived at the gym and we always go to our lockers to drop our bags and things before we re- turned to our apartments. But once we walked inside the gym, all the lights were on and our practice uni- forms were laid out nicely across the chairs. Coach told one of his assistants to tell us to get dressed. We were about to practice. This was late at night after an out of town road game. We got dressed and reported back to the floor and it was nothing but sprints. Everyone was upset and tired and didn't want to run. We were running because of me. I didn't care. I ran hard and i finished first. I refused to be broken. This was punishment and after the interview and how that transpired, I was on a mission to prove myself.

I lived Twenty minutes away from campus. When I had a few hours in-between class and practice, I would go home. I didn't get my car because my cousin was killed before he could buy it, but I had a rental minivan that I got from the agent who use to look out for me, and I use to park off campus so the coaches wouldn't know about it. I would go home to my Neighborhood courts and shoot around before practice and games. I didn't want to sit around and do nothing and let my mind float during this time. I was already mourning over my cousin, then my basketball situation wasn't the best either. I went back to my roots where I could just shoot around and lose myself. Before I went back to school, I stopped by to say hi to my moms and to my friends. My moms back door faced the alley where everyone hung out at. They shot dice, hustled and hung out there all night. My friends were asking whats up with my coach, they all watch and why he's not playing me. I gave them my story and I complained about how things were going and that I was tired of it. One of my friends said to me, you want to trade? I didn't think anything of his statement when he said it. But what he said next, changed my life. "You're complaining about being in college and playing basketball when I have people trying to kill me every day." That statement and question, changed my whole outlook and approach to my situation. At that point, my problems were no longer problems. I went back to school ready to kick some butt and thankful for the situation I was in.

Practice was different after this. I started to take it to another level and go after the younger players and other teammates. Coach use to get upset with me because he knew what i was doing. I wasn't doing anything out- side of what he asked, i was just separating myself from everyone and I wanted it to be known. He saw it and I went at them hard and didn't say a word. A crazy turn of events happened, when i woke up a few days later. I had an irritation in my scalp and had no clue where it came from. This turned in to what i would later call, "The BALD Head Game." I went to the trainer after class and she scheduled an appointment with the team doctor the next morning. We had practice that evening and a game the next day. That evening at practice, 3 players got injured. One dislocated his shoulder and the other two had ankle injuries. Funny how things happen. But i knew that i was in coaches dog house, in an inter- view he did a few games earlier, he said, "I like to pick on my players. It's Lonnie's turn, he's in the dog house." I didn't play the two previous games, but this game, all three players were our point guards. Myself and John were the better ball handlers left over. John was in the dog house as well. The next morning, i went to see the doctor and he advised me to cut all of my hair off so that the medication could go directly in my scalp. This was my first time ever having a bald head. When I got to the gym, I was late reporting because of my doctors appointment and the advisor was standing on the balcony watching me run in. She looked at me when i got to the top of the stairs and said, "you're always trying to be different. You wear the long socks, and now you cut your hair bald." I had an attitude, but i caught myself. I wasn't going to do anything to make myself the bad guy. I calmed my nerves and I said, the Doctor advised me to cut it off so i can apply my medication and I showed her the area of the irritation. She didn't pay any attention as I bowed to show her my hair, then she looked at me mean and said "go on." After I got my bags to head to the bus, before we left for the arena, Coach called me to his office and he wanted to see my head. I don't think she saw it when i told her and they didn't believe me. I showed him and then proceeded to the bus.

The bus was really quiet. Everyone had their headphones on and all I could think about was that he has to play me today. That was all that was on my mind. Once I got to the locker room and got dressed, we went out and warmed up for a little while, before we returned to the locker room. Coach listed the starters on the board, and neither John or I was starting. Our starting small for- ward was listed as our Point Guard. John and I looked at each other and shook our heads. As the game started, we both sat down at the end of the bench, still not sure if we were going to play or not. But that changed fast. Our fill in point guard turned the ball over the first three possessions. We knew it wouldn't be long before one of us got in. He subbed and tried someone else before he looked at John or me. The next sub came in couldn't run the point either. Then, he subbed John and I in. As I was going to the table, coach grabbed me by my arm and pulled me close and said something in my ear. What he said to me, turned my levels up another notch. I fought against it the whole season, but after this time, I had to rebel. Needless to say, it was the best game of my career at Georgetown. I finished the game with twenty four points, seven rebounds, five assist and five steals. We won the game 82-64.

Regardless of what happened after that moment, I was ready to step up to the table and contribute. You could imagine the mental and physical challenges I had to get through to still be able to play the game that i loved. But because I loved the game, I fought it. It was worth fighting for until I could better my situation. Also with prayers and God answering them, he made way for me to continue to be who I am and use the gifts that i was blessed with. After that game, I was never the same. When the players recovered from their injuries, they were back in their positions and I was back at the end of the bench. By this time, my mind was made up and I was leaving Georgetown. People on the outside felt that I should stay. The word was he doesn't play his younger players. That wasn't true because he was playing three freshman over me, and my teammates games didn't rise as they planned. It was deeper than basketball and a lot of ego and trust involved. I had to grow from it and keep it moving. All the things from this experience, I would carry with me to my next chapter. I was mature enough to check myself first. Make sure I was making the right decision for myself. I was talking to a friend about it that was a Senior at another school and he gave me good advice to think about. He had s similar experience but his changed because the school changed coaches. He didn't have to change. We talked about me transferring to Maryland University. After I spoke to him, as soon as I hung the phone up, my apartment phone rang right back. The school phone service was called "Hoya Net." Until this day, I strongly believe that our phones were tapped. When I answered the phone, someone said, "Coach wants to see you in the office. I went down to the office, and when he came in, he started laughing. He said, "you going to Maryland?" With a smirk on his face. Then it changed and got serious and he said, "no the hell you're not!" After our conversation, I knew that I had to go.

"I could play with the chains taken off in the summers." - Julius "Dr. J" Irving

Chapter XII:
Summer League

GROWING UP, WE had recreation basketball leagues and summer leagues. AAU basketball wasn't as popular as it is now. Only a couple teams back then. And on those teams were the best players in our area. Knew nothing about AAU. All I knew about was the Urban Coalition, Pro Am and Eddie Saah summer leagues. When i began playing in those leagues, it opened the doors to private gym runs with pros. I started playing at Doctor Carr, Maryland Univ., Mr. kitchen and a bunch of other spots. Working out for players back then was conditioning, weight lifting and getting shots up. That's it. You got better playing pickup games and competing all the time. That's how we developed as players.

Today I believe that training, Club, travel and AAU ball, has actually slowed up the development process. Kids are doing more of controlled things, instead of playing the game and learning how to play and move naturally. Kids are getting to college and struggling with things that require their natural instincts. So many come from situations where they are told to do this, move like that, do this, and when those aren't an option, they're loss. Basketball is a game of instincts and movements. Those things can't be simulated. It's no better teacher than the game itself. A few leak through the cracks and pick it up on the way. We have to remember the higher you go the numbers get smaller and smaller. From grass roots, to high school, to the pros. It's limited spots at the top. Those who pick it up the fastest get those spots. Most get comfortable during the gras roots years because it's so many options. But those select few that get it and are taught correctly wins in the end. It also takes some luck and being in the right place at the right time.

Having players to watch, play with and learn from speeded up the process. When I first went to watch the games at the Pro Am at HD Woodson High School, I had just started playing ball with the older guys and i use to catch the bus to North West D.C. to play ball at Shiloh Baptist Church. My Moms found out about their youth center after I had got in trouble in my Neighborhood. She wanted me occupied while she was at work, so i use to go across town and play with the guys who attended the center. When I first got there, I was unsure if I should be in this Neighborhood, because it was on seventh street N.W. by one of the hottest strips in the area. I had to walk through the strip to get to the church when i got off the bus. When i got to the gym, i'm sure it wasn't what my moms had thought. It was just an open gym of Neighborhood kids. When I walked in, i watched them play and a guy came to me and asked did I want to play next. I said sure and when our game came up, we played and we won every game. The guys we beat excuse was that i was tall. I was 6'2 at the time and i didn't use my height to my advantage. I just shot the ball and I was a good passer. I made a lot of friends up there and they told me about these other leagues on seventh street and the Pro Am at HD Woodson High School. I was traveling in uncharted territories where I shouldn't have been during those times, but as a basketball player, you get passes everywhere. Especially when you can play.

My friends at Shiloh took me to the games on seventh street and it was all kinds of pros playing out there and local legends who i did not know at the time. One of my friends brother was coaching out there and he told him about me. Hep me on his team for a few games, I didn't play much because the guys were much bigger, stronger and faster and it was a lot of money being bet during those games. But i loved my seat and i loved listening to the sounds and the dialogue of the game up close. These guys were some of the best players that I had ever seen before. There were college players and pros playing and I was a youngster and I was a part fit.

Our next stop was going to the Pro Am at HD Woodson. Here I would see one of my favorite all time players. He wasn't my favorite before I saw him at HD. In the NBA he was solid, but he didn't play the same. or should I say, he played his role in the NBA He was an amazing play- er. His name was John Battle. This was the best player that I have ever seen in this City! He was athletic, strong, had ball handling skills and was a lethal shooter. This was my guy. I watched him score eighty points and that was his average in that summer league. I use to go to the gym and copy his game how he attacked the bas- ket and used the mid-range. How he covered the ball in traffic, and used his leg when he jumped to shield players away. I was learning what the pros was doing with- out even knowing it. That was a new addition to my game. I didn't label it as that, mid-range and driving, it was what John Battle was doing and I wanted to do it. My curiosity was piecing my game together and making it complete.

Chapter XIII:
THE URBO

A FEW YEARS after, when my cousin was released from prison, he took me to watch the Urban Coalition. My first experience there, we were sitting in the stands. He asked did I think I could play out there and I told him yes. He knew the coach on one team and told him to give me a jersey and put me in. I went in and I was nervous. The gym was small and people felt like they were sitting on the court. It was loud and if you went out of bounds, you would run into someone. The first time i got the ball< i was near half court. Not realizing where I was standing, when i caught the ball, I just turned and shot it. It almost went in. The next possession, I turned the ball over. My cousin yelled "you ain't ready," and told me to get off the court. Told the coach to take that jersey back. That was the most embarrassing moment of my life. I hated that feeling and I never wanted to feel that way again.

The Urban Coalition was the best summer league of all time in Washington D.C. It was where the grown men played and the areas finest. After i sniffed what it was like as a youngster, that was another lesson that took me to another level. I knew I could play with those guys, but I didn't overcome the nervous energy. It got the best of me. When I returned, It was different. I'd experienced so much and my confidence was on another level.

This time around, I showed up to the Urbo to do work. Melvin played on a team and said I could play with him. He was my point guard and the best floor general at the time. He taught me a lot about playing on that level. We played games on the blacktop, at Lorton penitentiary and we played for the Legendary Madness Shop in tournaments all around DC, MD and VA. That Team had DC Legends Bootney Green,

David Butler and John Turner on it as well as myself and Melvin. I was use to playing with Melvin and was comfortable playing anywhere. I grew as a player playing with him. The game was so easy playing with other players that could really play. From the start, one player could never guard me man to man. I was looking past my man at an early age and see- ing where the help was coming from. That was one of the things I earned from the older guys in my hood. So by the time I got to play in the Turbo, everything was isolation. Man to man on an island. This played right in to my style.

I was playing on a team with Melvin Middleton, Curt Smith, Bootney Green, John Turner and David Butler to name a few. That team would be considered as a stacked team, but every team was stacked back then. The games were played with NBA rules and time with four twelve minute quarters. The clock stopped on everything. It was enough time for everyone to be involved. My first game, was fun. We were blowing the team out and putting on a show. My job was easy. All I had to do was shoot jump shots. I was making them left and right. So much time on the clock, I was making seven to ten threes a game. The crowd was saying "Water Hose"

when i shot the ball and making a sound "ooooooooo- OOP" every time I would shoot. That just made me want to play more. I was looking forward to the weekends at the Urbo. The energy from the crowd was the best. If that didn't motivate you, then I don't know what could.

After a few years, some of the guys on the team was old- er and after we won the Championship they fell back and I began to move to the forefront of the team. I would have more ball handling responsibility and get more shots. Our team was younger now and I was one of the top players on the team. I was getting majority of the shots and the iso's. I was having a great summer and my name was buzzing around the city as a must see, but my break out game came when a team came with a bunch of NBA players and their team was loaded. This is where I gained the love to play against the best and not with them. My team didn't have any pros on it at the time. But one particular player who was coming off a great college season at Michigan, came and showed out. We weren't checking each other because he was a big man. He told the show by throwing a pass to himself in transition off the backboard from half court. The ball hit the backboard hard, "BOOM" then bounced and he caught it around the free throw area, took one dribble, then windmill dunked it. Everyone ran on the court and it stopped the game for about five minutes. It was wild like that. They let the crowd express themselves however they wanted to.

As the game continued, I was out in front of the fast break with no one ahead of me. I called for the ball and the pass came late. By that time, i ran under the rim and didn't realize it. When i received the pass, I jumped to dunk, not knowing how far under I was, and got hung on the rim. The ball hit the front of the rim I came down and jumped again to lay it up. When I was running back down court, my friends were sitting behind our bench and laughed at me, along with the rest of the crowd. I started laughing too. I told the both of them to "bet fifty dollars, if I get the ball on the left side, I'll take it be- tween my legs and dunk it on the fast break." Immediately they took the bet. A few plays later, I got the ball on the left side, but it was in a half court set and I was being defended. A double team had come from the base- line side. I faked to go middle, then turned back baseline from that left wing. As I was driving to the basket, I saw a clear path. All of a sudden, I attacked the basket hard and thought this was my chance for the dunk. I took one hard dribble, then I took off. A defender had went by me and reached for the ball as I took it through my legs. The same player that had just threw himself a pass off the backboard, jumped. He tried to block it and I dunked it. Nobody saw that coming, and I didn't see the defense. I turned to look at my friends because I won the bet, and the whole crowd ran on the floor. I don't remember how much time was left on the clock, but the game was over. Nobody had seen that dunk live before. That was one of the many crazy things that I have done in the Urban Coalition.

As the older players stopped playing, we started picking up more players and the team was still good, but the chemistry wasn't the same anymore. After winning three Championships and everyone knew who the top players were, the younger guys (I was young as well, but I had been established already) started to make names for themselves. Sports agent Len Elmore got a team in the league and had the biggest all star roster ever. They had the NBA number one draft pick that year Joe Smith, Rasheed Wallace, Walt Williams, Sam Cassell, Jerry Stackhouse, Xree Hipp and more! We were play- ing them and we added a new player to the team and all of a sudden, my playing time and touches were cut. We were losing and one of the pro's came to our bench and asked, "what is he doing on the bench?" I was wondering the same thing. When the second half started, I started and got subbed fast, and then that same pro player from the other team, came to me and grabbed me and when I stood up, he pulled my jersey up over my arms and head and said, "if they're not going to play you, you can come and rock with us." I was pissed off and I had been play- ing with that team for awhile to throw shade and play a new player over me. I went on the other team that day and I gave my team former team the business.

I had another shut down play when a loose ball was bouncing towards half court and i was chasing the ball down against another opponent. he swiped up at the ball and the ball went about tenet in the air. I jumped in the air to go get the ball and got my hand on it still airborne, while doing this, i glanced around and saw Xree take off and point to the rim, as I was coming down and was near half court, I split my legs in the air and bounced it between my legs hard. It got to the rim and Xree caught it and dunked the alley oop. That play was crazy and shook the house. After that, they gave me the ball every time down so I could go at my former team, and I went to work on them. The Pro player, was hugging me and walking me around to the crowd saying and pointing with his other hand, "he's a Pro! He's a Pro. He's a Pro!" That game gave me a new anger towards my opponents. Who genuinely cares about you in this game? Who really want you to shine? The same way my teammates switched up on me, that same guy "the Pro," that embraced me, later on switched up on me when I became a threat to him.

After that experience, one of my friends, "Big Will," started coaching and built his own team and played in different Summer Leagues. When he started that, I was his main focus. It was all about me. I didn't have to worry about who's on the team, y shots or my minutes. I wasn't a selfish player. I did whatever I needed to do to win. Even if someone else was hot, i was make sure they got the ball in positions to be successful. If i had to guard the best player and make him guard me back. That was my advantage, because while they were worrying about the matchup and going one on one, i would do things to ware them down and pick their team apart as well as get the win. A lot of players couldn't do both. They would concentrate on scoring. That was the measure. Who scored the most. I would score, but I would put so much pressure on them on both ends, they would get caught up in the battle. If I got scared on, I would hurry up and get the inbound and attack with all intentions of making a play. Didn't have to score, although i would a lot, but i would keep my teammates involved so they would remain happy and compete. I've won a lot of games and a lot of battles against a lot of good players.

My goal was to win first, and don't let the outshine me. If they got a dunk, I would make sure I got a better one so you would forget about theirs. If they hit a three, I would back up and shoot a deeper three. If they made a good pass, i would out do that. It was competitions within the competitions. I would win most of those battles because I had guard skills at my height and the guards couldn't jump like I could. Players my size couldn't handle like I could. And most didn't have the instincts or the range that I had. So I would win those battles and win the games. Year's later when I was playing pro ball, my teammates who played with me for the first time, use to say I had the Cheat Code. I play like I'm playing a video game. And that's how I felt when I played. Basketball was never hard. The politics around the game was.

The Urban Coalition was the most competitive league our area has had. I was a part of a team that won a lot at the Urbo. Winning three Championships and not having one NBA player on the team was a big accomplishment. The league was full of good players from top to bottom. Baltimore was one of the toughest teams in the league. We played them in the Chip two of the three times that we won it all. One of those Championships was one of my best games ever. Not because I scored Fifty Three points, but because I did it in game that was really challenging. Physically and mentally, it was one of the toughest games that I had played in a Summer league, but I it made me rise to a level that catapulted the rest of my career. They were so strong, strategic and played team basketball with so much talent. Our team played the iso game and we took turns scoring. We had the best scorers who could play that style and still make it work. That league gave me the most confidence and mentally had me playing on higher level by the time it ended. That was the league that all leagues will always be compared too. It's abrupt ending, left us with no closure. It was moved to McNamara High School in Maryland, but couldn't carry the essence of D.C. basketball with it. It wasn't the same and didn't last long after the move.

Chapter XIV:
KENNER LEAGUE

WHEN I GOT to Georgetown, our Freshman team played in what was called the Eddie Saah Nike Summer League. Our team was called "The Tombs." The Tombs is a restaurant that's on campus and have been sponsoring the team for years. We had six freshman on the team and we would add other players that wasn't Georgetown players. This was while we were attending summer Freshman year orientation. We stayed on Campus and took classes, had workouts and played pickup at the gym. The summer league was a time for us to get to know each other and play some ball. Get to meet our fans and let them see a glimpse of what was to come next season. We had a really good team and gave the fans what they wanted.

After leaving Georgetown, and attending Northeastern, I have grown so much and matured as a player. My new Coach Dave Leitao had just came from UCONN and had coached quite of few players beefier me that went to the NBA. He brought in a system that highlighted my mid- range game even more. All the things I have learned over the years were adding to all the raw skill that I had. Before Coach Leitao came on board, I sat out and practiced and played with the team that was full of New York, Maryland, Baltimore and D.C. players. Everyday our pre-season games and practices were intense and it was little beefs going on between the players because of where we all were from. This was more competitive and personal than anything. It was Pride Ball.

When I came back that summer, all eyes was on me. I had to sit that season out after I transferred. So this would be the first time that anyone would have seen me play in over a year. I worked on my body and I still had to practice with the team. When I walked in the gym, I wasn't welcomed or greeted nicely at all. I took it upon myself to speak to my former teammates and coaches and got a lot of cold responses and no eye contact from a few. I didn't need anything else to motivate me because I was already motivated to show them what they were missing. That return game, I had 40 points at the half. Hitting shots from everywhere and making it look easy. When the second half started, my coach told me he couldn't put me back in. I didn't understand why, but he said while we were warming up at half time, someone came over and coach said said to not play him anymore. I grinned and sat on the bench for awhile to see if he really wasn't going to put me back in and he didn't. The crowd was asking why he's not putting me back in, I just shrugged my shoulders with a smile, then i got up and grabbed my stuff and went in the back to change my clothes. After i changed, the game was still going on and I walked over to coach to shake his hand and didn't get any response from him. I left and wouldn't return for a few summers until I finished school for good.

Every level I have played on, I experienced all kinds of adversity. Regardless of the outcome, it has never interfered with my performance. The one thing that I always knew was that I was there to play basketball. That's what I loved. If I did my part, how can it be overlooked. I had no clue about power and politics and I really didn't care. I just wanted to play basketball. After I spent the next few years in Boston for school and my summers there playing ball, I returned home on a mission. I had a Chip on my shoulder. I felt the tension from a lot of the players and people that I played with who weren't there from the beginning. They respected me because I could ball, but didn't like me because I was different. Players hung with each other and did things together and I didn't. I hung with the guys from my Neighborhood. Some didn't like my confidence and took it for being cocky. I was miss understood.

While I was in Boston, I worked out and prepared for my upcoming season. I hung with the locals and got on their basketball scene immediately. I played pickup games in gyms, recs and local parks. Got in fights and physical altercations as if I was a local. Boston was a big part of my basketball journey. From my time in Boston, I got to know a lot of people. A few of my guys played on a team that traveled to New York to play. I got to hang out in the city and go with them and watch them play on a team called "Biv 10." It was Michael Bivins from New Editions homegrown team of all Bostonians. I didn't play, I was just going to watch. They were playing in the Entertainers Basketball Classic known as the Rucker, at Rucker Park. I heard of the Rucker, but had never been there to see it or experience it.

The love was totally different in Boston then it was back home. Outside of my neighborhood in S.E., my school friends and the older hoop eras of D.C., I could feel the difference from the others around the game when I re- turned. I was different. My swag was different, my confidence was different and I had met so many people in between that time who were celebrities and staples in our culture. I was a basketball star! I was known around the country by basketball fans everywhere and I was just finishing college. All because I could play basketball really well and who I am as a person. I got along with everyone. I was the cool D.C. dude.

My friend Big will had his team in the Kenner league when I returned home that summer, and I was one of his featured players. Will and I stayed in contact when i was at Northeastern and he use to look out for me and make sure that I was Ok. Plane tickets were seventy five dollars for a shuttle home on student fare, and my schedule at the end of the season was the best. I didn't have classes on Monday's or Friday's. so when i wanted to come home, I could leave Thursday after class and fly home and be home Thursday night until Tuesday morn- ing before my first class. Almost five full days. I had that option every weekend. When I did come home, it was just to see my family and hang with Will for the week-end, hang uptown and hoop. This time when I had returned home, It was two years after my first return to the Kenner League and now I was finished College. I was staying in New York and playing in their Summer leagues and I would come home on the weekends to play with Will in the Kenner League.

The Dinner League now, had a lot of rising young players. This was different from the Urban Coalition. It was time for a New Era to be ushered in. And as always, I was there for the top competition. My number one goal was to win. After that, it was about entertainment for me. I loved the attention and the things that came with winning. I was a Nike player at the time from my relationships in New York. Every time I got to the Park, the rep was there with a bag with a fresh pair of shoes. One pair I remembered where the hightop gold Foamposites with no laces that zipped up in the front. I was the first to debut those and I couldn't wait to get to DC to play with them in the Kenner League. That night it was a huge game and perfect for my return.

The team we were playing against had a crew of All NBA players. Steve Francis, Moochie Norris, Jerome Williams, Sam Cassell, Al Harrington and others. I didn't have any NBA players on my team. This game was an eye opener to me and my friends were diss pointed although we won. There are always things that we don't see while playing that spectators can point out. During this game, I was locked in, it was my return and I want- ed to show out. The stands were packed on both sides and I had never seen it this packed since Allen Iverson made his D.C. debut in the same gym. McDonough Are- na. The practice home of the Georgetown Hoyas. This game was so big that Coach was also there in attendance. The whole city had come out for this. I wanted to to show out for this one. My New York friends came down with me for the game, I debuted the Nike Foamposites which became a popular shoe in the DC Metropolitan area, I was playing on the Roc team coached by Jay z, I was a Roc-A-Wear Ambassador and we were playing against the best team in the league on paper. I was on a high and I was ready to backup all the talk that i was hearing when I was away. Other players and people around the game were saying I think i'm from New York now, because I took advantage of opportunities that were in front of my face.

The biggest issue that I had with that is, I didn't think those outside of my circle had the best interest for me and I what I wanted for myself. They wanted me to be there for them, and that was selfish. People are happy when you're there for them and entertaining them, but didn't really care about what was best for you. I love to entertain, but when it comes to fun and surviving, you have to do what you have to do to survive. New York compensated its players very well and showed the appreciation for your involvement. DC you played for the competition and bragging rights. I would play when I could, but I had a job to fulfill in New York. If i had a game in both on the same day, I would go to New York, I had to eat! I wanted to get paid and I did.

When I arrived to D.C., I met up with my guys first be- fore we went to the gym. I always showed up with my friends. It's just the essence of showing up with your new tat made these games better. It was a part of the en- trance, a part of your personal show. And in those days, the doors were usually closed and people were outside and couldn't get in. So, I would roll up with my crew and everybody with me would get in. I liked showing up right before the games, because I didn't like to get into all the talk and he said she said before I played. I had already heard what trash talk I needed to hear before I showed up. The barbershop talk spreader fast and my phone use to ring everyday with messages of what someone said. So this game, I was matched up with Steve Francis, because the first time we played, I hit the game winning three pointer on him and he said some things to my friends in the stands, that added more hype to this game. I was on a high and I didn't even care who was on the floor. It was a bunch of pros. Everybody could play and we knew that each of us were going to do their thing, but i wanted to win more than anyone.

I guarded Steve and got up on him regardless of his quickness, size or skill set. He was a Point Guard with a lot of moves and an explosive player. I knew I was to tall for him and a problem for him in the post, but I was go- ing to play his game and make him guard me on the other end and dish back whatever I received. It didn't turn out quite that way because his teammates would help him and double team me, an have strong weak side help. That didn't stop me from getting my thirty six points and the win. Yep, as stacked as that team was, we won the game. It was showtime that whole game. Some crazy plays being made, ankles being broke and I was even a victim of probably the move of the night, but it didn't stop my mission. That just made me come harder and get the job done against that team. One of my friends use to bet on most of my games. Especially the big ones like this one and would give me some of his winnings with- out knowing that he had bet on the game. He would even do this when i was out of town. When I left that gym that night, I didn't want to hear anything else from anybody about debates or comparisons to anyone else. That team had everybody and we got that Win, that's all that mattered! Looked good doing it with those exclusive gold foamposites on.

Chapter XV:
The Farms

W E WOULD FIRST ride through Pomeroy then Birney place. Then to Eaton rd and chill out there for awhile. You can see everybody walking down the hill heading to the games. I would walk down the alley to my friend Keith Davis house to get juice and use his bathroom. His back- door was steps away from the court. You could smell the mixture of aromas in the air. The sun starts to go down, and as it starts to get dark, you can see the smoke rising from one section of the court. When I get to the gate, I would first get my dinner from the chef out the back of his truck, then say whats up to my guys playing cards on one of the outdoor generators as soon as you enter the gates. You can see the scorers table over the lawn chairs sitting around the court and like clock work, the MC and Commissioner of the Goodman League, Miles would announce, "The L Train is in the building." I would put my fist up to acknowledge the announcement, then make my rounds and dap all the people who i recognize and have supported me as long as I have been playing down there. I have played in all eras of the Barry Farms Goodman League and I have seen it grow from a neighborhood league, to a local league, to a nationally known league featured on NBA2k and mentioned on sports outlets everywhere. I grew up with the league and have played longer than anybody in the league.

Growing up in Southeast DC, was a time you had to be there to experience. There were beefs in your Neighbor-hood and beefs with other Neighborhoods in near by walking distance. At the time, Barry Farms was a place if you didn't live there, you weren't welcomed around there like the other places in S.E.. East of the river or Anacostia as they say today, Southeast is a difficult place to travel to and the Neighborhoods are traps to enter into and get out. So we didn't have many visitors un- less you were visiting with someone who lived in one of the neighborhoods. You couldn't even come visit a girl or your cousin if nobody recognized you immediately! For me, my introduction to the Goodman League was my cousin, Wayne Edelin.

The first time I experienced the Goodman League, the league was for the neighborhood players only. No out- side players could participate. Although I lived in southeast, I wasn't from that side and i wasn't allowed. I use to go watch my cousin when he played and one of my all time favorite players at the Goodman League Sutton played on his team. I knew Sutton because he used to come up Malcolm X and play. He was an older real smooth ball handler that could pass with great court vi- sion and shoot the lights out. He was always fresh when he played and drove nice cars. I loved watching him play. He and my cousin played together and it was fun watching them. My cousin at that time was a little chubby. He was already short, so he soon retired from playing. But he could shoot the ball and had a good IQ.

One day I was on Eaton road hanging out with guys and they decided to let me play. It was towards the end of the Summer before their playoffs started. Wayne didn't want to play and they only had five players. Needless to say I played and had a lot of fun out there playing with them. I didn't try and do to much, because they didn't really have a lot of tall players on the team we were playing against. I was an obvious mismatch, so I rebounded and passed a lot and helped us win the game.

The following year, two of the guys I met hanging with Wayne down The Farms, Kenny Wing a guard that was athletic and could score in bunches and El Moe a PG that was quick with handles and a Floor general, needed a big or tall player to run with them. I was down there so much with my cousin, they allowed me to play. I was cool with that because I loved to play and would play anywhere. That year, the league started changing. Teams started adding players that weren't from the neighborhood and the games moved to the other courts on the other side. We turned out to be a lethal team and won the Championship three times straight. That's right, a three peat.

A few years later, while I was away in College, the league still continued. When I returned, my former teammates had retired from playing, then I started my own team. That summer, I met a couple of young guys that I had hooped with hanging uptown with my guy Big Will. Their names were Lil E and Sheik. They were two hungry young cats that played hard and played defense and was down for playing against whoever and whenever. We use to go around to the gyms where the top players in the city would play and wreak havoc on everyone. I remember when North Brentwood was one of the top places to play. It was a community center on the border- line of N.E. And Brentwood Maryland. All the top ballers from D.C. would go there to play. D.C. recreation centers didn't have gyms, so when we weren't playing outside, we would go to Maryland gyms in the mornings to play. D.C. rec centers were inside schools and we had a few that actually had gyms, but they were used for other activities. We couldn't play in the schools until the evenings but even then we liked playing outside instead.

The runs use to begin at 9am. If you got there late and had to wait to play, you probably would have to wait an hour to get on because it was so crowded. So one person had to get there early to get on the list and the rest could come at 9 because our spot was secured. Or if you were that good, people would hold a spot and pickup the best players. One day I went down there and I took my youngins with me E and Sheik. Not many of the guys knew them because they were younger. But one game we were playing against a team that had three of the most popular players in the area on it. We went head up and matched up with them and knocked them off. Everyone was asking about my young guys then. I brought them down the Farms when I started my team.

Next I needed a Coach and my best friend Lavelle, use to hoop in the evenings with some guys he knew in Mary- land at Temple Hills recreation Center. He would go all the time and asked me to come with him. I would go sometimes just to get some run and pass him the ball so he could do his thing and make sure we won games so we could stay on long and get some good run. The Farms was above that level of play so he came on as our Coach. My friends I met uptown had there own store called "Chocolate City," they were our first uniform providers. From my days with Big Will, having fresh uniforms and sneakers was always a must. I had to have a fresh pair of sneakers every game. Always wanted to have what nobody else didn't. After we got the team started, Velle finished filling out the roster. During this time, In the summers, I missed a lot of playoff games while I was in school and once I finished other basketball obligations, when I could I would show up. It was not until I was done playing profession- ally that I would be able to be there and finish out the summers. It sucked, but my pro career and money was more important.

As the league expanded, more of the top players started playing in the league. More well known figures in the area started getting teams from all over the City. The league opened the gate for those who wouldn't usually come to Southeast. Barry Farms was a great location because it was at the crossroad of a interstate and a parkway that lead to all parts of the city and area. You didn't have to go deep into Southeast for the courts. Interstate 295, Suitland Parkway, South Capitol street all lead to roads to get everywhere.

By this time, we transitioned to A new Sponsor, "Shooters Sports." Rob the owner went to the same High School as I did, "Eastern," and he use to travel to NY to watch me play at the Rucker as well. We made Shooters famous in New York. I was playing with Murder Inc. at the time and Irv and Chris Gotti both represented and wore the Shooters brand. We had friends in Harlem wearing it also. Rob and Velle were both my guys and we stayed fresh in multiple Shooters uniforms. Once I signed with And 1, I would get sneakers for my whole team.

We had a good run with Shooters making deep runs in the playoffs and going to the Chip almost every season. I had a lot of epic games at the Farms as the league continued to get better and better. Being from Southeast, I loved where I was from and represented it wherever I went. I love DC but I loved my hood in Southeast more, Congress Park. Congress Park wasn't a place and still isn't, a place for outsiders to visit or hang out at. So when opportunities from sponsors that I acquired at And I, they wanted to support my efforts in the City by giving back to my communities. I couldn't leave my hood out and although we didn't have a open league for out- siders, through Western Union, I was able to get Congress Park and Barry Farms basketball Courts refurbished. We did the announcement and ribbon cutting at the Farms because the local news and other media out- lets were coming, and since the Farms was where the league was, it made more sense for our sponsors to get their visibility there. With the new baskets and newly refurbished court, players are always excited about that and the league took a new turn for the better.

Miles the commissioner was the best MC with his timely and witty commentating. He embraced the culture of DC and became his own show. As well as spectators came to see the games, they came to see Miles. He created his own brand and made the league even more attractive. He changed Summer leagues in D.C. Barry Farms was the place to be. You had the "Season ticket holders," who sat on the floor seats around the court and brought their own lawn chairs. Then there was the "smoking section," that's self explanatory. The "BF Crazies" the neighbor- hood people who lived in "Barry Farms" the "VIP's" and then your regular spectators. The Farms had grown and was a must see experience. Regardless of what was go- ing on in Southeast and that neighborhood at the time, crime stopped for a few hours to see some great basketball.

Once I started playing with AndI. I would miss a lot of games being on Tour and traveling the Country. When I could get home to play I would. While on Tour, we would fly to cities a week before the game to do promo on the media outlets. Before the DC game, I flew there early along with a few of my teammates and asked Tony Jones aka Go Get It to play with me down the Farms. I wanted them to see him play and how high he could jump and his dunks. We went out there and put on a show. When I returned on Tour, I had an idea, and I spoke with management about us playing down the Farms against the top players in the league. It turned out to be a great idea. The game was set up and we even got And 1 and other sponsors to sponsor the league. On the And1 side of things, we met and incorporated that game as a part of our tour and featured it on our DVD, The And1 Mix- tape Tour and the TV show.

The game was promoted and advertised on DC radio and by word of mouth. When we arrived to the game, it was crazy! People came from all over the City to see us play. I played with the And1 team because I was under con- tract and it was one of the biggest outdoor summer league games in DC ever! The Goodman League had jumped to a National stage. Following that up, I spent the summer in ATL playing Summer League with Stephon Marbury. A few years after, he stared his own Brand and debut his new sneaker. He wanted to come to DC and advertise his sneakers. Again we set up a game of players from New York this time to play against the Barry Farms select team and Steph showed up with trucks with 50 cases of sneakers that he gave away for free. Everybody in attendance got free "Starbury" sneakers that just came out. Another win for the Goodman League and our area. Being a part of this league as a player and a contributor made me feel good about our community and not being around as much as I wanted to, because I was traveling and playing on tour and be- ing a gun for hire. I would be on call and go anywhere to play and get paid for showing up.

In the Goodman league, I was a showman. I played to win, but I gave the people what they wanted to see. I talked to the crowd before the game, during the game and after the game. It was fun. Basketball is

supposed to be fun. That doesn't mean smiling and joking and not being serious, it means having joy in doing something you love. I was out
there to destroy and embarrass whoever. My thing was to outplay
anyone and make it look easy. That was my way of separating myself.
When a player was talked about as being good, whenever I was matched
up against them, for some odd reason, people would pick the other
player instead of picking me. I could never figure that out. But when we
lined up across from each other, it was game on and talking couldn't
save them. Those games would wound up with me being double teamed
, or the player I am supposed to be competing against, not guarding me,
or the player would get straight up abused on the court.

As the years went by, l left the team I started because of a few
differences. I was then playing on Jay Z's team at the Rucker "S. Carter"
that was sponsored by Reebok d Jay Z. He created the team to promote
his new sneakers, the S. Carters that looked like the old Gucci sneakers.
Since I was down with the Roc, I called my team *The Roc Boyz." We
were coached by my guys Taz and KC ...... , and we were the show! We
played the prime time game every week, matched up against the top
teams. Miles would play our theme song when we were about to play,
Roc Boys by Jay Z, "..the Roc Boys in the building tonight, oh what a
feeling I'm feeling life!" This song would pump me up. It put me in a
space full of energy because at that time, I was at the height of the street
ball culture globally. I wasn't just a local player in my neighborhood. I
had created a name for myself globally. I was one of the best players in
the world, and this song would remind me of that.

In most of my summer league games, I would get double teamed
regardless of who we're playing. That was too my advantage because I
played to win. I wasn't trying to get 40 points unless it was a marquee
matchup, which usually looked like me against a NBA player. I've had
my matchups against quite a few NBA players at Barry Farms. The
biggest ones were against Gilbert Arenas and Kevin Durant.

During the lockout, Kevin would frequent the Farms and play everyday on different teams. He just wanted to get the bump. I was in New York at the time and one of my friends and former coach Lavelle use to always tell me about a kid that was going to Texas that played down the Farms. I never got the chance to see him in High School or at the Farms, but I did see him at Texas. He was a special player. I was mostly impressed with his poise when he scored, that's a major signal of a true scorer, not pressing but a shot maker. Years later I would come home and play down the Farms and every- one wanted to see that matchup.

The first time that we played against each other, I had heard about a game he had played against a player from Baltimore they called "P-Shitty," They had a shootout and one of the classical games at the Farms. Even after that game folks talked about how he has been dropping 40 on everybody and how deep he was shooting his jump shots. So when it was my turn, everyone was expecting the same thing. I had a little fuel added to my fire because one of my friends had the nerve to say, "don't guard him. Let somebody else guard him." That pissed me off. At this time I was about 37/38 years old and he was a young NBA player, and the season after that summer, he would go on to get NBA MVP.

Hearing my own friends doubting me and later saying it was because the age difference, pissed me off and just gave me more reason to go out here and show this crowd what they already knew, but just had to be reminded. I remember this game well because of my emotions. I had to calm myself down, so i smiled and cracked jokes with my spectator friends so my emotions didn't get the best of me. I was really pissed at the guys who doubted me. Right after the jump ball. We got a quick two points. Kevin went to get the ball, but when he turned around, he wasn't expecting me to be sitting right there. I picked him up '94' feet. This 30 wasn't going to be easy for him. When he saw me, I saw his face and he knew I came to play. He gave me a move then we raced down the side- lines and he got by me and drove all the way to the rim and got a dunk. I could hear people on the sidelines say- ing "I told you." But they didn't know what I knew, and that's why I was out there to show them. The next three possessions, the same thing. A foot race. He was going to shoot it every time and I knew that. So I kept picking him up full court. He scored, he turned it over, he got fouled. Thats how this was going, but, there's another side to the game. He couldn't guard me either. The difference was, I wasn't making it a one on one game, I was making plays.

The games were physical and some people on the side- lines by their bench didn't like what was going on and were making comments about how physical the game was getting. They felt I was being a little too aggressive, and I call it not letting a player do what ever he wants. Fouls were being called and you only get six. The referees at the Farms protect their guest players, so it was more of them not liking the outcome rather than the physicality. I didn't let him come down and just shoot jumpers in my face. He had to work for them and people weren't expecting that. We won the game and went on to win the next four matchups against his teams. He scored his thirty points and I scored mine and we got five wins.

One of the most epic games was against Gilbert Arenas. The first time we locked horns, we came out the victors and he showed up alone and played on a team that was a regular team and just added him as an extra player. The same thing happened this game, it got physical. I guard- ed Gil and I do this thing on defense that I have mastered, when a player drives and get by me, when I go to block the shot, i swipe fast right over the top of their head as they are raising the ball up and make contact with the ball. Players hate it because it's close to their head and it's uncomfortable. But I make contact at least half the time. He started getting frustrated and then started running full speed right into my chest as if to run me over and they would call the foul on me. Then i started bracing myself and it was like football. At the end of the day, I came to win and in the middle of a one on one battle, I still play team ball. We had the league and I had an argument with their bench because it's things like that, I love. I'm a trash talker, before, during and after games. I love it. Gilbert got so upset that he kicked the ball over the fence onto the highway. We got that victory and was on to the next. Our next time play- ing, Gilbert came back and this time he was accompanied by a few of his Washington Wizards teammates. Caron Butler and Deshaun Stevenson. I had played against Deshaun before in Miami during the Andı tour. He and Rayful Alston showed out that game. I got a scar on my arm tattoo from Deshaun. I just got the tattoo and it was fresh. I had a bandage on and tape over it.

Somehow he ripped it off and made a long scratch through the tattoo. It actually still healed properly eventually. But at the time it was still there. I guess they called the Hounds in for this epic game. Their team was stacked with NBA players and local top players like Tre' Kelly, who was young and putting his stamp down in the City after having a great college career at the University of South Carolina. Tre' had run off a series of 40 point games in the city that summer, and this would be another one. We had our same team of lo- cals and no additions, and this would turn out to be the matchup of the summer. As the game started, we were all standing around for jump ball and it felt pre-deter-mined that Deshaun was supposed to be guarding me as he walked beside me and said, "I got this." That is so dis- respectful to me. When someone makes it their point to say it out loud that they're guarding me, makes me feel like they really think think they can. I always had a saying that goes, "If I am a good player, your defense has to be better than my offense." I knew that wasn't possible. And that was how I treated it.

This game was a barn burner. It seemed like it would never be over and the fouls were lopsided. They didn't want that team to lose. We were hitting on all cylinders and I finished the game with 45 points. We went into three over times that game and i fouled out at the end. We split with that team after taking that loss. It was a fun game and greet experience.

I just knew we would win because it wasn't enough balls for that team to go around, but the three overtimes worked in their favor.

Growing up and playing outside with my friends and the older guys in my neighborhood, prepared me for this competition. We had athletes of kinds in my neighbor- hood. Small and fast, tall and big and big and strong, we had it all. We also had guys that were as talented as the NBA players that I have played against over time. They just didn't have the focus to chase that dream. A lot of them we lost to the streets. But those experiences pre- pared me for the direction my life took me. I didn't have the long and great NBA experience that I wanted, but I had a great basketball experience. And basketball it what I loved more.

Watching the Goodman league grow from a neighbor- hood league to one of the greatest summer leagues of all time, is a testament to its commissioner and its players, and i was there for it through the whole process. Three eras. My last go around, I actually retired and became a coach. A youth basketball coach and the time it required, kept me from working out and playing ball. All my time was spent on developing the kids. KC one of the a coaches from the original Roc Boyz squad, was still coaching and had a young team. They were struggling and hadn't won many games and were in last place. They had a play-in game to make the playoffs. He called me and asked me to run with the squad and I still had an itch to play, so I said yes and joined the team. I know that I'm competitive and wanted to win, but I told myself that I was just going to go play and not do to much since I hadn't been playing.

This is now a new era of players and the game is totally different. I was out there looking like the old guy, setting screens, getting waved off, setting screens off the ball and they wouldn't use them, it was whoever got it shot it. No team ball whatsoever. I subbed myself out the game and said that I was tired. Really I was blown by how we were playing the game and didn't want to play anymore. Then I looked around at my friends and the people who had came to see me play, and knew that that couldn't be the last time they had seen me play and go out in this manor.

Although I didn't work out or play ball anymore, I rode my bike daily around the city. I rode it everywhere I needed to go, so I had a little in the tank and could push myself. I checked back in the game and took over. I became the floor general and put the young scorers in position to score and make it easier for them. I became the decoy. Since I had the ball, teams would pay attention to me and I started picking them apart. My teammates was scoring at Will.

This worked throughout the playoffs. This last place team was now in the Championship. What a way for me to bow out. I hadn't won a Chip out there in a decade and I missed a lot of games in the gap between that and my retirement, but to return and have a chance to win a Chip at the Farms and walk away, would be an ending to a great Chapter. That game was special because a lot of friends came back to see the game because they heard what we had pulled off. Then some came to see if instill had it. We didn't get the job done. The team that beat us was a much better team and I wasn't the younger me who could take over games and get it done on my own. I wasn't in shape for that and my body had let me know it. It's no shape like being in basketball shape, and this was one time that I had experienced that and was disappointed. But like the say, you don't have to get ready, if you stay ready! That was my last game at the Barry Farms Goodman League.

Chapter XVI:
BEANTOWN

M Y LAST DAYS at Northeastern ended early because the
school was on a quarter system. Once my classes were done, I went to
New Hampshire and played in a Professional League before the NBA
draft workouts began. I had a few months before the draft activities
began and a few of my Boston friends were playing in this league. I
finished the league on the All Tournament team and was co-rookie of
the year with Michael Lloyd from Syracuse University by way of
Baltimore. I had competed against Mike back at home in summer
leagues. One of the best competitors I played against. That year we were
dazzling crowds up North with our DC and Baltimore styles of play. We
were in the top 10 in almost every statistical category.

I left before the season ended to go and play ball in other cities to
prepare for team workouts and the draft. Play- ing with my pro friends
and learning what I could and getting the knowledge of the game from
them would teach me and prepare me for camps and workouts. My
agent at the time was a young guy from Connecticut who was hungry
and worked really hard at contacting teams to get me on their radars. He
had his license to be an agent and everything was official. At the time, I
really wasn't concerned about an agent, because I thought that my game
would speak for itself. I also did my part on the court winning games
and posting solid numbers in college, my pre-draft pro league debut was
good as well earning co-rookie of the year and making the All League
team. But something wasn't right. All the scouts and coaches knew who
I was, they knew my talent and skill level, but the responses we were get-

ting were weird. The responses had nothing to do with basketball. I would find out later how narratives work and politics. To me things start with a word, that word becomes perception, once that's created, then it's followed and become the story to everyone in that circle. Perception goes a long way, specially in tight exclusive circles. I was being judged by a lot of things that I had no clue about until years later. A security officer that use to work for the league, who would work directly with players talked to me at a club one night and gave me some insight on the word that was going around the league about me. There has been so many stories going around, that I had to stop listening to them. I had to lock in and focus on the things that I could control. One of the biggest things was that D.C. players were pre-judged by the players before us. We inherited all kinds of stereotypes. A few were that DC players were hard heads, they don't want to leave home, they will up an leave and return back to D.C., and they are trouble makers. Coaches thought this about players from our town for a very long time. This is what the guys before us left us with and in the minds of coaches. But none of those things were relatable to me.

Before I made it to that point, I transferred to North- eastern from Georgetown University. My first season as a Husky, I could practice but I couldn't play in games. It was OK for me to play in local leagues around Boston without committing a violation. I was familiar with the basketball scene in Boston, I played in the Boston Shootout while in High School a few years before, and the Boston Team had some very good players. Boston has a very big Urban community in neighborhoods like Roxbury, Madappan, Mission, Orchard Park and Dorchester. It was also home to a lot of great high school, College and Pro players. Dana Barros, Casey Arena, Wayne Turner, Jamal Jackson, Bevan Thomas, Trent Forbes, Fudge, Roscoe Patterson, Rick Brunson to name a few. It also had it's hood superstars as well.

The bad sections in Boston were just like the hoods in other cities. I wasn't expecting that because I saw the Boston they showed on TV that was white and had an accent like Italians. I got to know about the real Boston my first day on Campus. In 1993, Starter jackets were popular and everybody wore them back in DC. It didn't have to be your favorite team because some jackets looked better than others and you wore them to match your sneakers. I was wearing a Pittsburgh Steelers jacket with some black and yellow Air Force ones. Two guys walked up on me and said, "Yo you with the Steelers?" I didn't know what they were talking about, but I was from the streets and I knew they weren't being nice and didn't think I played football. So I used my hood basket- ball card fast and told them, "look man, I go to school here and I'm here to hoop and that's all." They respond- ed, "word?" with a little excitement in their voices be- cause after I told them my name, they heard about me from an article in the local News Paper about North- eastern's new transfer from Georgetown, which was me.. I thought it would be easy to know that because I was so tall. But it's a lot of tall bangers in Boston that also hoop, so size alone won't get you a pass. After that encounter, we walked in the same direction and I stopped at a pizza shop on Huntington ave on the cam- pus. They came in and we talked for awhile and I learned a few stories about Boston's basketball leagues and it's urban culture. It was a lot of leagues going on in the Winter.

Before the season started, I use to play open run on campus with the students and other athletes. I loved playing pickup and since I had to sit out for a season, I needed to take my frustrations out on someone on the court. When I played with these guys that consisted of students, athletes and non-students that were friends of students, I treated them like they were the enemy. I was angry and had to take my frustrations out somehow. Basketball was my escape and the only way I could cope. I didn't abuse any substances, nor did I have anything to do but go to class. So my victims were in that gym.

I wouldn't hold back anything. I wanted people to leave the gym and go and tell people what they saw. I wanted them to know that the new dude in town was a monster. And that's what i did. I made sure every player that got in front of me knew the difference. I didn't want any questions for anyone who i've played against, to ever be able to say, he's just all right. Or even think we were equal. I dominated them. One of the students that played, live off campus and told me about a couple of his friends that were ballers who could play and knew about some local leagues. I was down for whatever and would play anywhere. That was my thing. I would have went to Beirut to play if the word was they could ball out there and the money was right. That was just me. The friends he spoke of, I was familiar with one, and I had heard of the other. Trent and Fudge were their names. These were two of the best players in the area and they both played Division I basketball. I got with them and started playing in the local leagues.

These leagues were good. It was a lot of older players and semi-pro players and hood players in these leagues. They were really competitive so I could bring it every game, and bring it I did. The Coach that I played with, had a team called "BG." He called it BG because his favorite colors were black and Gold. The Coach name was "Chill." Chill was a cool guy that had an appearance like a Pimp. He had just got out of Prison in 1992. Lived in Franklin Hill, Mission, Dorchester and Roxbury, so his hood pass and credibility stretched beyond the parameters of Bostons projects and hoods. He drove a Black Mercedes with a 14k Gold colored kit and Gold BBS rims. He wore Black and gold clothing, gold chains and gold rings, and his hair was in a curl. Chill was a cool cat, but was serious about his coaching and winning. Once I joined Chills team, a movement begin. We started winning all the tournaments including the money tournaments and leagues as well. We played in everything. During this time, i put my stamp in Boston. I became a house hold name.

The more we played, the better the team would get. When the summer hit after my first year in Boston, I stayed to take Summer classes. I visited home and brought my six year old nephew back with me to live for the semester. Taking care of him was fun and I had a lot of help. My friends were four young ladies from Connecticut who lived below me and they would keep him and care for him while I was in class or playing ball. I got him a puppy, to even keep him more occupied and to have company that had the same energy he had that could play with him as much as he wanted to. The Freshman players also stayed for the summer and I told them about the teams and they would play with me. The games were so much fun playing with my teammates mixed with the local guys and winning these tournaments. Chill had built the "BG" Empire from those teams.

During the same summer, I met a few guys at a club, they saw me playing in one of the tournaments and told me they had a team in the biggest Summer League in Boston. It was their outdoor league just like the leagues we have in DC and around the country. It was called "The Malcolm X League." For short, "The X." The league was at Washington Park on Malcolm X BLVD ran by a guy named Dave who use to play in some of the indoor leagues we played in and was a referee. Dave told me about his league before, but i just thought it was just an- other league around town. The guys I met called them- selves R.S.O. They were one of the biggest gangs in Boston. They drove Bentley's, Range Rovers and wore gaudy jewelry. That's what people did in the 90's. RSO was lead by Ray Benzino, he was the guy I met and was the Coach of the team. He was also the headliner of their rap group with the same name title RSO. These guys were known all around Boston and had a big reputation in the streets.

Benzino and I had a mutual friend as well in New York. He was a partner with the Source Magazine and I knew the owner at the Source from a Mutual friend. I also use to be a hired gun to play in Money tournaments for the Source as well. Boston as I learned upon my arrival, was no different from any other urban City. It had it's sections that were just as rough as anywhere else. All the teams were based around different sections of the city and all were ran by street cats that would build their teams. The games at The X were for bragging rights and high stakes. The dope boys from the respective gangs and neighborhoods would bet on the games. The league had a lot of talent. It had the OG's who were Boston leg- ends, it had College players and local favorites. I took my entertainment style to The X and performed. The Park was the spot to be. It was the Summer time hang- out. All the dope boys, finest women and most popular people would hang out there. Some didn't come to watch basketball. It was the weekend spot. It reminded me of how Crenshaw in L.A. was in the late 80's and 90's. Pull up with your crew and hang out.

I became the instant must see at the Park. Whenever I would play, the court would get crowded. I would show off my skill with my moves, deep shots, fancy passes and unorthodox dunks. Not many have seen a 6'8 guy in the streets with the skill set and entertainment I provided. I was a showman that could entertain and win games. But a lot of the players didn't like that. Some players felt that i was trying to show them up. Honestly, that was definitely my plan. I never wanted a player to think he was on my level or could do the things that I could do. If you hit a three on me, I'm going to shoot a deeper three on you. If you hit me with a move, i'm going to out do your move. If you dunked, I'm going to dunk right after you and make it look easy. That's how I played and I was going to help my team win the game. In one of the games, I came down in transition and split two guys while spinning and took the ball between my legs and dunked it. When i landed, one of the guys pushed me into the pole. It was after the play and wasn't a basketball play at all. He was frustrated because I was showing off. One of the RSO guys that was on the bench ran on the court and punched the guy in the face and continued swinging until he got pulled off of him. Ray (Benzino), told me don't worry about nothing, just keep doing you, we got you. Another time I was playing and a fight broke out for the same thing. I played through all the PHYSICAL play and the fouling because I was use to it and I could still get my JOB done in those types of games. But it was good to know I had PROTECTION be- ing in another city in their hoods hooping it up with money on the line.

The highlight of the league was the MATCHUP between our team RSO vs Mission Hill. Mission, had the best team on paper. A few of the guys I can remember, were really good from MISSION. Jamal Jackson (RIP), was one of the best players in his class in 1993 coming out of High school. Jayson Edmonds was an athletic player and one of Mission Hill legends. And Frankie Patton was a really good Point Guard, I liked his game a lot. He use to get it done. They were undefeated and had the best team in the Park. But we were here to change that. Dave the commissioner waited until late on the schedule for that game to be played. The first time we were supposed to play it rained. Whenever either team played, the other team would be there to watch. They saw what I could do, but they didn't believe it could happen to them. Good players mindsets are all the same when it comes to hooping. You have to show and prove in the game of basketball. Regardless of what you see someone do against someone else, you still have to experience it for yourself. Playing is not the same as watching. And that's what happened to Mission.

When we finally played, it was a late evening game. The whole block was packed. The cops were out there heavy, the cars, the people, it was the biggest game of the summer. Both teams were fully loaded and ready. I could hear the best going on and all the tension. The feeling for me was intense. They were a really good team. They were blowing teams out. This was the test. Although Mission and RSO were rivals, they had a street respect for each other. But you had to see this. It wasn't like the Rucker where you had rappers and their hoods on the sidelines. That felt more like a movie. This was hood. You had two different gangs and hoods on the same side of the court together and you know every last one of them was strapped. I was a chest piece. the outcome of this game either way was on me. The pressure was on! I embraced it! I loved these situations where basketball was in the middle of a tense situation. I knew it was possible that something bad could have happened, but the excitement and the adrenaline both tries to take over you and give you feelings of fear, nervousness and jitters. I learned to embrace them all and use them to drive me. I worked to be in this position and now it's time to show my work.

At the start of the game, Mission players were being very PHYSICAL. Like everyone, they saw my frame and my relaxed style of play and thought i was weak. So they bumped me and pushed me, double teamed and roughed me up. But they were playing right into my hands. I knew at some point they would get tired of be- ing physical, the game was close and they would get COMFORTABLE at some point. I lead my team by facilitating and getting my teammates going. i played good defense and rebounded the ball and created. The Mis- sion players played together and Frankie had them CLICKING on all cylinders. They were running and FINISHING, getting dunks and putting up numbers. We were right there with them. Our coach and bench was getting frustrated. Arguments started breaking out and the game started getting intense. By the half the game was still close and both teams were getting tired. We were in a good space, but our coach didn't think so. He went off in his SPEECH and it was more about not los- ing to them than playing basketball. With all of the money being bet and the street BRAGGING rights on the line, It was no way we could lose this game.

The second half showed the fatigue setting in on both teams. It was hot outside and the humidity still lingered when the sun went down. It was now my time. I was in the best shape, I wasn't tired and I was ready to go. It was SHOWTIME! I began to takeover. I started making threes and we got a comfortable lead fast. My shots were falling and it was over in my mind fast. Regardless of the score, I was on. When you're in a comfort zone and you're playing hard and everything you're doing feels good and it's working, game over! Chalk this one up and they knew it. They started fouling me and then one of the fouls was not a good basketball play. Then both teams left their benches. No fights broke out just a lot of talking. The commissioners cleared the courts, we continued and we won the game. They told me to go with one of the guys immediately and get out of there. As we were leaving the court, gun shots started going off from outside the court. It was other guys watching the game that got in to it. It was so many people out there you couldn't see where it was coming from or who was shooting. People were just running everywhere we. We made it to the car and I got back to campus safe. We continued playing the rest of the summer and it was more shootings and fights every weekend. Thank God I made it out of that safely and with a Championship.

Before my time ended in Boston, my last year of the three, I started playing for a Twin named Foster. Foster was another guy that just loved the game. He was more like the modern day teams where he would have his team play in all the Money tournaments in the city and outside the city. We would travel around the area from Connecticut to Providence to play in money leagues. I was doing this all summer long and Foster made sure that I was taken care of, win or lose. We won most of the time and he would break the winnings down. I've never played in so many money tournaments ever like I did in Boston. We didn't have any in DC. Guys would bet and win lots of money, but Boston had tournaments that you could win a pot all the time.

Chapter XVII:
ATL Pro League

I MET STEPHON Marbury in New York after competing against each other. Towards the end of the Summer, players start preparing for next season. I went to Atlanta for the summer with Steph and we worked out at Georgia Tech every morning, just weight lifting. We hooped in the Atlanta Pro-Am that summer. I never heard of that until I went there with Steph. This Pro-Am was full of NBA players on every team. A few of our games, we had the Barry brothers on our team. Brent and John Barry. they were both in the NBA at the time and very good players known for shooting. The first game we played there, the Barry brothers didn't play. We were actually short handed and one of my friends, music executive Breyon Prescott stepped in and played on our team. Breyon is from Washington, D.C. as well and was living in Atlanta at the time. He was a good player but wasn't known for playing basketball. The first game I played was against a player from the Philadelphia 76'ers who had just got drafted in that summers draft. As expected but never understood, people couldn't understand how this guy who's not in the league, is embarrassing a player that is. I use to wonder that as well until i learned about the business of basket- ball. Our next game the Barry brothers were there and we played against a starred team of NBA players. I didn't change the way I played the game because I was there to show what I could do. That's why Steph brought me there. He passed me the ball often and I shot it often. One of the Barry brothers asked Steph, "who is this guy taking all the shots?" Steph responded, "He's official, he can do that." The respect I got from Steph, not only to bring me to Atlanta to workout and play with him, but also to be confident enough in me to allow me to stand out front and showcase my game, spoke volumes about his character and assisting me in getting prepared for the league. I averaged 40 points a game in the three games I played. From that, I got other opportunities in Atlanta. I re- turned another time as a guest to play for Ludacris in a game he had for charity against Bad Boy. I will always remember that game because Diddy actually came in the game and tried to play and I hit him with a. Move and he tried to tackle me. We had a quick scuffle because he knew he was wrong, but he didn't want to get embarrassed. I also would fly to Atlanta and hang out with Jermaine Dupree. J.D. was a cool cat and I played in a few games for J.D. as well. The Hip Hop and basketball connection was very strong. Players loved hanging around entertainers and entertainers loved hanging with players that could flat out hoop.

Chapter XVIII:
Pro Life

It's funny how in life, labels and titles tend to have us play those roles. When I became a pro player, my mentality and approach to the game had changed. I felt like a pro, and I adapted the pro lifestyle. That whole process is learned. My first experience as a pro happened after I left Northeastern and went to New Hampshire pre-draft. My agent thought it would be good for me to play there while we were waiting for the draft events to take place. I was out of school early and had a long time before that process would begin. The team was in the USBL and called the New Hampshire Thunder- loons. I made the All Conference team and received Co- Rookie of the year.

After New Hampshire, my next stop was the Orlando Magic. I had an achilles injury that happened in Philadelphia at the Bakers league before I got to Orlando which limited my time on the court. I made a pit stop in Chicago before Orlando to rehab and I got the opportunity to work out with Tim grover and Juwan Howard. When i arrived in Orlando, It was about a month before camp started. I was staying with Dennis Scott who was a big part of me being there as I went undrafted. I followed his lead and he showed me the pro lifestyle. Before the injury, we hung out at his home in Virginia a lot. We hooped every day and worked out with Mr. Kitchen and Grant Hill. Mr. Kitchen and Dennis helped me polish up on my shooting and get some kinks out that was making me a streaky shooter. They picked up on it right away. Dennis is one of the most pure shooters of all time. He is another player that made it to the league after being a prolific scorer at Georgia Tech, then was limited to a role as a shooter in the NBA. Roles happen to the best of us.

Camp was a great experience. I got the chance to see how guys like Penny Hardaway, Dennis Scott, Nick Anderson, Brian Shaw, Darrell Armstrong, Gerald Wilkins and Horace Grant prepared as professionals. Coming off the achilles injury that summer before, I had a special pair of sneakers I was testing for Nike that I received in Chicago. They weren't actually basketball sneakers, more like cross trainers, but they were the first pair of Nike sneakers that had the air bubbles that went all the way around the sneaker from front to back. I wore them to take away some of the traction and pressure from my achilles. And on top of that, I would put on numbing cream applied with gloves, before I got on the training table to get taped over my socks. I would also wear a ankle brace over the taped ankle. My foot felt like I had a cast on. When we got closer to pre-season, Penny, Gerald Wilkins and Brian Shaw were all injured, so I was left to go head to head with Darrell Armstrong the rest of camp. Darrell was a hard nosed hungry guard from North Carolina that attended Fayetteville State. This was his fourth year in the league and he was playing for his contract. He had yet to get that big guaranteed con- tract that the other players on the team had. So I caught a real lion during his feeding time. He would pick me up full court the whole day everyday and it felt like he even followed me back to the training room. I was so over- whelmed because I had never played the point this much and had to get the ball to veterans when they wanted it. It was no time to fight with him and not produce on time. I grew up and became a better player playing against Darrell. Even though I had all these great players around me, my battles and challenges with Darrell in practice was what made me a better pro. After dealing with Darrell, I could deal with anyone.

One day in practice, we had a scrimmage and the injured players were on the side watching and the game was in- tense. So much trash talking and pushing and egos fly- ing everywhere. There were so many competitions on the court and off the court in that lockeroom. I remember one player driving up in a 500SL Mercedes convertible with a loud system, that same week three other players would drive up in the same car with systems just as good if not better. Donald Royal won that battle when he pulled up in the gold 500SL kitted out with the crazy system. They competed at everything. In this game, i handled and controlled the ball on my team so i had opportunities to show what i could do. I earned Darrell's respect, and he backed off and stopped picking me up full court. I was thankful for that because I hid the back pains and the muscle soreness and the fatigue in my foot from the achilles. My body was struggling but i couldn't show it because I wanted to play.

We were on offense and I called a play that consisted on a sidelines pick and roll, when I came off the pick, the two defenders jumped me for the double team, my instincts kicked in and instead of picking up the ball and passing it out, I spun threw the double and took the ball between my legs while splitting them, attacked the basket and threw a behind the back pass to the cutter who was Devin Gray for the slam. Horace Grant ran from behind and grabbed me and picked me up and Carried me off the court. The news cameras were in there and got it on video and ran it in their sports segment. That one segment made me a favorite in Orlando. My Mother came to Orlando to be with me and helped me get settled. She loved the city and the weather. When we went to the mall, everyone would stop us for autographs and talk to us. We would go to stores and shop and the stores would tell me to grab more stuff, it was on the house. We would go to dinner and the waitress would tell us our bill has been taken care of. We didn't have to pay for any- thing. In return, all they wanted was a hand shake and a thank you. Next was our first scrimmage against each other. Players were still hurt and we were playing in front of the fans. Again I would play well and make an amazing play. Running for a loose ball with another player, he dove on the floor to grab the ball, but i slapped the ball down and made it pop up. While the ball was coming up, I jumped over him and took the ball around my back. When I landed, we were close to the corner, I gathered myself and stepped back behind the three point line and shot the three. I made the shot and the fans went wild. After the scrimmage, we hung around and interacted with the fans and they were excited about the season. Some of the fans expressed that they really loved watching me play. It made me feel good and my confidence begin to rise.

In pre-season I didn't get a lot of time, but I saw Charles Barkley in a hotel and he remembered me from George- town. My friend and Sixers star Allen Iverson came to town and we hung in the hotel before we played and both had started to let our hair grow, and decided we were going to race to see who's hair would grow the fastest. The injured players returned and I saw a few minutes against the Pacers. I got the chance to guard Reggie Miller for a few plays. I learned so much in such a little time from him on how he set the defender up and use screens because he was doing it to me. Then we played the Clippers and I subbed in as a point guard. I was ready and it was much easier than playing against Darryl Armstrong. I had a few highlights that made sports center. I belonged here. When we went back to practice, I was really gimpy and my foot wasn't holding up. I finally had to reveal my injury to the trainer and I did just in time. He said I was lucky that I didn't completely tear it. But the bad part was that it was going to take as much time to heal because it didn't completely tear. That was my last time playing. I remained in Orlando for the season and returned to D.C. when the sea- son ended. When I got home, It was one of the toughest times of my life. I was torn, depressed and feeling sorry for myself. I remember during pre-season, Allen and I was having a race to see who's hair grew the fastest. i completely let it go and that's when I started wearing braids. My sister would do my hair when it got long enough so I wouldn't be sitting around looking pitiful. I watched Martin everyday and the laughter helped me make it through. I wouldn't leave the house because basketball was all I wanted to do and I couldn't play anymore.

I stayed in Orlando for the season and returned home the following year to recover and get back on track. I came back to DC and used the Run N Shoot pickup games to get back in the swing of things when I could play again. I had no lift from the foot with the injury. I couldn't jump a foot of the ground. I just ran up and down the court not being too involved and practicing jumping off that foot until I could fully jump again. Even at Orlando, I made it through camp and pre-season without jumping. It took two whole years before I was ready to play again. I wasn't on a team at the time, so I had to rehab the old fashioned way, play until i was ready to join another team. My next stop was Delaware.

The Delaware Bluebombers was an ABA team. I needed to play in something to get footage to prove that I was ready to play again. I couldn't get in a high level league because I didn't play for two years, so I had to start from the bottom. This team only paid fifty dollars a game. We had games every weekend and I would go the day before the game to practice. I didn't go to practice during the week because the team didn't pay for housing. When I would go up on the weekend, I would rent a car and pay for my own hotel. My travel expenses were more than what I was making to play, but I needed the footage.

This league was good for me because it surprisingly had a lot of good players in it, and the league was scouted by overseas scouts. I would pass up on overseas offers be- cause my focus was getting back in the league. That sea- son was really good. I came back jumping higher, running faster and because of all the work and rehab I was doing to strengthen muscles, I strengthened muscles I never had before. I returned in the best shape ever. My cuts were better. My footwork became better and my reaction time was also faster. It was time to make a strong push.

The following Summer, I would return home to play for the Washington Congressionals of the USBL. Coach Mike Mcgleese from Dunbar High School DC was the head coach. This was one of the best teams in the league and represented with some of the best local talent in the city. On this team was Greg Jones, Moochie Norris and Curt Smith, three of DC's Finest. Curt lead the league in assist while myself and Greg jones lead the league in three pointers made and percentage. Moochie was the glue piece that brought the IQ and made sure we were all on the same page. This team was amazing to watch. We were picked to win it all but fell short when in the semi finals we lost to a New Jersey team coached by Hall of Fame Rick Barry. Unfortunately, Moochie and Greg caught a flat on the drive to New Jersey and missed most of the game. We were short handed and came up short and lost the game. Afterwards, my close friend Lavelle who had traveled up to watch the game, asked Rick Barry what he thought about my game. Rick said to Lavelle, he's a really good player, I would have to see him play when someone like Scottie Pippen is guarding him. What I took away from that was pure flattery. For him to throw out arguably, the best defender of all time in the same breath as me and my favorite player of all time, gave me a high that mentally put me in another space. I already believed that no one could guard me, but this just put the icing on the cake. Any defender lined up in front of me, my thoughts were, "You're not Scottie Pippen."

This was just the beginning of my USBL experience. One of our games, we played against the Pennsylvania Valleydawgs, this team was coached by Darryl Dawkins. Hall of Fame Boxer Larry Holmes was one of the teams owners. That game I made twelve three pointers in a win against probably the second most talented team in the league. A few players the Valleydawgs had were Dominique Young, Kwan Johnson, Ronnie Fields, Tony Rutland and Ace Custis. That team was a fun team to watch and play against. That following Winter, I went to South Dakota to play in the NBA. When I returned, I started the season for the Washington Congressionals and Darryl Dawkins called our Coach to trade for me. How the league worked back then, you couldn't hold a player back from leaving, especially when the pay in D.C. wasn't good. The teams owner didn't have a big budget for the team. or at least I wasn't seeing the money. I left for Pennsylvania for more money and because Coach Dawkins had bigger plans.

The Winter before I went to Pennsylvania, I played against Coach Dawkins in Winnipeg Canada in the IBA. While I was in Canada, we all hung out and he told me about his plans further than the USBL and the IBA. It was a new league forming, the rebirth of the old ABA. It was paying six figures and he would be the Coach of the Tampa Bay Florida team and he wanted me to come with him. So his plan was for me to come with him in the summer in the USBL Pennsylvania Valley Dawgs, then continue on to Tampa for the ABA. He made it happen. In the beginning of the season after a few games, I was traded to Pennsylvania. For what i don't know. That season in Pennsylvania was one of the most fun seasons ever for me. When I arrived to Pennsylvania, a game was in action and my new team was playing. They gave me a uniform, I went in the locker room and got changed and came out and sat on the bench. Watching my new team was so exciting and fun. I couldn't wait to get in the game. Once Coach Dawkins subbed me in, It was showtime. We had a big lead on our opponent and the guys welcomed me by passing me the ball almost every time. They had a big crowd much bigger than the D.C. crowd and the team was a big deal there. I showed them how much I was happy to be there during my first break away dunk in transition, I took the ball between my legs in the air and dunked it. No one was expecting that. That was my gift to them. In 1998/99, nobody was doing that dunk in game. That was just me, I was never afraid to do something I knew I could do in a game. Confidence creates success. Confidence makes it all work. Positive thoughts produce positive results.

Now Coach had put together a team that was ready to make a run for it all. With the roster that was already there, then adding myself and Ronnie Fields, it was truly something special to watch. We were getting two thousand fans for a USBL Summer League game. Even if you weren't a true basketball fan, you had to come and see us play. Families enjoyed watching this team play. After each game, we went to Larry

Holmes sports bar for dinner and to hang out. It was the spot to be after the Valleydawgs games. We would hang and eat with Coach Darryl Dawkins and Larry Holmes and listen to stories while eating and having good times. Families were invited, their were autograph sessions and after that was done, it turned into a twenty one and over club.

Playing on this team was right up my alley. A bunch of talented guys that could all score. Even tho we had two really good point guards in Dominic Young and Tony Rutland, I was a facilitator and the glue piece who could change his own game to make it all work. I was the Scot- tie Pippen of the team. Kwan, Ace and Ronnie were all big time scorers, I just did whatever the team needed to win. Whatever Coach Dawkins needed from me, I delivered.

AFTER THE USBL season ended, I would go on with Coach Dawkins to Tampa to play in the ABA for the Tampa Bay Thunderdawgs. This was the league who would allow us to stay home and not play overseas. The money was good and I was excited because this was going to be my second highest payday playing basketball after experiencing NBA paychecks. The league had a lot of big name players who were stars at some point on their college teams. Also it hosted former NBA players who were looking to get back into the league. The expanded from the East Coast to the West Coast with teams in L.A. This league was probably the best league that made a lot of players aware of me on a national level. I was a completely different player than what they had saw from me in college. Still playing with my same friends form the Valleydawgs, we also added two more of my friends John "Franchise" Strickland and Kerry "Goat" Thompson. Both are legends in New York basketball scene and they brought a totally different style of play to our team. They made us even more exciting and a tougher team to beat.

Still with this team my role would be similar, but as the competition in the Winter got better, I had to raise my level of play and be a more aggressive scorer. Coach Dawkins told me one day, that I was the most talented player in the league. It's time for you to show it. He kept his ears in the NBA Circle and the word was that I was an exceptional offensive player, but I didn't defend like I play offense. I didn't like when I heard my defense in question because I would always take the challenge of guarding the best player on the court. Not totally under- standing how i could play defense like I played offense, I accepted the challenge and focused on my defense. Personally I saw that as another excuse for whatever reason to hold me back, I didn't allow that to hold me down. I always believed that your defense had to be better than my offense to stop me, and that was pretty impossible. So how could my defense be as good as my offense? Was I supposed to tone my offense down, or raise my defense up? I raised my defense up. I would be tops in the league in steals and blocked shots while excepting the challenges of guarding teams opposing players. That still didn't seem to be enough.

After we received our first four full checks, the league started having financial problems with such big payouts because the attendance was very low at the games and the games were held in Arenas. The teams were in locations mostly that didn't have NBA teams. Also Los Ange- les was one of the few teams that had a team. Once the money starts looking shady, players start to vacate the league. Some of us held on as long as we could in hopes that things would be corrected. Me, I was trying to get back in the league and I was another step closer. I was in the conversation again after overcoming injury and adversity, I couldn't stop. Then Coach Dawkins told me about scouts from different countries that were interested in me and he said go get your money. If he gets an opportunity, he would be leaving as well. I took his ad- vice and moved on to South America.

After the first summer I spent in Pennsylvania, I moved on to the IBA (International Basketball Association). The IBA was another professional team with teams located in the Midwest. My team was in Rapid City, South Dakota. If you have never been to Rapid City, it's a popular city in South Dakota located in the Black Hills mountains. Rapid City is the home to the famous Old West City "Deadwood" and Black Hills is where one of the greatest tourist attractions Mount Rushmore sits. It's called the town of President's because of the Bronze statues of Presidents in downtown Rapid City. Small rural town in the mountains. but I enjoyed my time there.

This trip to a new team showed me something many didn't know, but around that time, every team was talented. Each time I got to a new team and league, I saw that the talent was as just as good as the next. One thing that allowed me to keep my separation was to play my game and not play like everyone else. For some reason in these leagues, it seemed like the players have been playing together overseas and in pro leagues often and they all seemed to play the same style of ball. I was the odd ball because I never conformed. This team had a different feel to it. I saw what another level of play looked like. These athletes were different. My teammates were Mark Young, Kipp Simms, Jermaine Walker and Kevin Rice to name a few. All very athletic scorers with a gritty style of play. These guys really could get at it. They talked trash and we all were alike and had a great bond. The chemistry how we played and how we competed was amazing. This season took place during the NBA lockout season. The NBA was calling up players from every league at the time. Also in the league was really good players like Sean Colson from Philadelphia who we competed against. He lead the league in assist and was in the top 5 in scoring. Sean would get his 10 assist in the first half before going off in the second half and getting thirty. First time I saw a player get at it like that. My former teammate for the Washington Congressionals, Curt Smith played in the league and a player from Chicago Mac Irvin was also in the league. This was a re- ally good league. The IBA got me back on the NBA Radar. I posted huge numbers over a months span that were amazing. Teams took notice and I would get workouts from multiple teams during that time.

I left Rapid City and went to the Lacrosse Bobcats in the CBA (Continental Basketball Association) to play for NBA Legend and Boston Celtics Champion Dennis John- son. On that team was Dontae Jones the Mississippi State assassin who had one of the best NCAA tournament runs that I had ever seen. He was a a prolific scorer with explosive athleticism and a mid range game. I had just left Milwaukee working out for George Karl and Terry Stotts for a week. Coach Karl wanted me to play on the Lacrosse team and if the Bucks had an injury or a spot, they would call me up. I didn't wait around for that because the team in Lacrosse was so stacked at my positions, Coach D.J. played me at the power forward position. I was 6'8 205, that wasn't going to work out for me. That was the second Time I was thrown to the wolves. I went to a mini camp for the Sixers and I was guarding Power Forwards there as well. I would play whatever I need to play realistically, but those were place filler positions. Those teams had no plans on keeping me. They had their contracts in place and took me because I was sent there from other coaches and agents. I figured out how that works later on in my career. When you got caught up in the CBA and NBA pool, politics plays a big roll.

I landed with the Baltimore Bayrunners in the IBL (International Basketball League). My Coach was a familiar face, Herb Brown. He is the brother of Larry Brown former head Coach of the Philadelphia 76'ers. Herb was a good Coach for me. A lot of players didn't like him be- cause of his style of Coaching. A lot of veteran guys felt like he treated us like College players. A lot of pro players don't like coaches that are hard teachers. I was use to it. I played for one of the hardest in College. Coach Thompson. One of my teammates expressed his dislike by punching a hole through a chalk board after one of our games when he and coach had an exchange of words.

My teammates were Shante Rogers, Kirk Lee, Jamar Greer, Mark Blount, Rodney Elliott, Labradford Smith, Keith Booth and one of my favorite players all time, Lloyd "Sweet Pea" Daniels. Lloyd was a vet and

the OG of the squad. I was a big Lloyd fan and playing on a team with
him was one of my greatest professional highlights. He was the best
shooter that I've ever seen or played with. His range was deep and he
could get it off standing still with a defender all over him. He would lean
his shoulder in to create space and then shoot and it was money. He was
older at this time, so he never practiced. He would come to practice and
stretch his hamstring the whole practice and get shots up. He took me
under his wing and gave me some scoring tricks that I still use today. It's
amazing the little things and messages shared by players who have
experienced a lot of basketball. He shared with me the things he's
learned and someone shared with him the things they learned and so
on and on. Thats a part of development. Giving back the knowledge that
you've gained from your experienced and pay- ing it forward. That's how
we make the game better and maintain the integrity of the game by
having former and older players giving their knowledge to the next
generations.

Baltimore was a fun experience as well. All of the teams I
participated on were fun but they were all different with different types
of players, ages and styles of play. I lived in Ellicott City while playing in
Baltimore, I didn't want to take that drive everyday to Baltimore for
practice, so they put me up with the other out of town guys. Baltimore is
a basketball city and we had great fans. Most of the fans knew me from
the D.C. vs Baltimore games, so I was welcomed as if I was one of their
own. Most of the players were from Baltimore and were all local legends
that had great college and overseas basketball careers. I've learned a lot
from a lot of different players. The Baltimore players like Kirk Lee I
knew from playing in the Urban Coalition. He had the league record
dropping 90 points in a game. He was one of the best shooters I had
seen. Shanté Rogers was a really good point guard who lead George
Washington University to their best ever NCAA Tournament. Rodney
Elliott and Keith Booth both played at Maryland University as well and
were good players also. LeBradford Smith has a great career at
Louisville and good NBA career. He's now known for the infamous

Michael Jordan story when MJ created a lie to get mad at LaBradford so he could destroy him the next game they played against each other after LaBradford and the Bullets had beaten the Bulls the game before and LaBradford out scored Mike.

My journey through all of these leagues taught me so much. I am glad that it happened on the professional level and not early in my career. The wealth of knowledge that I had received, could only come from players and coaches who have experienced other players and coaches on these levels. I was blessed to have played for some amazing coaches through college and the pros, I also give credit to my grassroots coaches for the fundamental work and development. But this pro level was another story and this Baltimore team was one of the biggest memories.

IT WAS ALL kinds of drama on this team. Keith Booth and Herb Brown had differences and Keith left the team. Keith also played with the Chicago Bulls and have a NBA Championship. Lloyd who is one of my favorite players was playing mind tricks with me. I was the younger more skilled version of him, but he was tricking me into not playing my game, so that he could get his minutes and play in front of me without practicing. That was the first time I experienced a vet move like that. I didn't take it personal when I realized it, I already knew that this level was a dog eat dog world, but he would get in the coaches ear every time I made a mistake and tell him to sub the young feller out which was me. But what he didn't know that I was too mentally tough for drama and spear headed it when it arrived. If I wasn't playing the right way and he was, I just played how he played and did it better. That was my solution. So if he's playing the right way, then I'm playing the right way. Herb liked me and I learned a lot from him. But eventually he was gone and we got a new Coach. The new Coach came in and his philosophy was like playing 1970's basketball. He was easy manipulated by the older players and they started running the team. We started losing every game regardless of the talent that we had. It was Difficult to fix and that season was rough. I learned another thing from that team. The team is as good as it's leaders.

When the Summer would come around, I was back in Pennsylvania playing on my Valleydawgs team with Coach Dawkins. I needed to have fun again. Basketball seasons are the same as our weather seasons, it's more fun in the sun. I was back with my guys and we had an amazing and fun season. We were all back from our winter teams and players had a different mindset and we were making it happen. When Coach Dawkins first talked to me about coming to play with him and that we were going to also play in the new league in Tampa, it started after the Summer of 2000. One of my best sea- sons and I was close to going back to the league. But when the money started being an issue, coach told me to go ahead and take one of the over seas offers and get your money. That year the Super Bowl was in Tampa and I wanted to wait until after that before I left. So I stayed a little longer and gambled with a few contracts and some were off the table. At the time I wasn't sure anyway where to go, but after losing some of the offers, it made my choice simple. I wanted to go to Venezuela.

I agreed to go to Venezuela because I just wanted to see what the country was like. I also wanted to go because of the things I have heard about it when I mentioned it to friends. It was a beautiful country with beautiful people and amazing beaches. The Coach there told me that the majority of the teams we played were on a beach. I couldn't wait to get there. Before I left for Venezuela, I had a two week period before I had to arrive, I went to Miami to hang out with some friends. I've only been to Miami twice before that as a player with Georgetown and had lots of fun. It was close and I had to fly from there to go to Venezuela, so I went to Miami instead of going home. I also had to get my passport and back then, you could get a passport in one day in Miami. This was my first time experiencing Miami on another level other than as a college basketball player. I really enjoyed myself and wanted to come back and explore it more, It was time for me to leave. When I arrived to Venezuela,

I immediately felt like I was in a different world. The police were all around the airport and carrying their guns. Not concealed, but in their hands. Dogs everywhere sniffing for contraband and I stood out like a sore thumb. It was people complaining that they have gotten robbed in the parking lot, American people and I immediately thought to myself, where am i really?

Leaving the airport on the way to my residence, we had to drive through the mountains. It was one of the most beautiful views of a city I experienced. We were cloud level and i could reach out of the window and touch the clouds. All of this was stopped by a check point with officers holding M16 rifles. They were looking in the car and asking the driver if he had any guns. The driver told me that police in this country rob people as well. I really started to second guess my decision. So far the start was shaky and I was just leaving the airport. As we continued around the mountains, I started seeing the rural liv- ing areas. It looked like wood boards and sheet metal stacked up on top of each other to create living quarters and they were stacked up in the Hills. This is what true poverty looks like I thought. It reminded me of the pictures that I had seen on TV of how Africa was portrayed to us by the media. I couldn't under stand how people could survive these living conditions. As we got closer to the city, i could start to see buildings and hotels and structures that looked more like what I was use too and it was clear that it was two types of liv- ing that were separated by the hills and mountains.

Once we reached the city, it was hectic. Lots of people walking, cars on the road and the traffic lights didn't seem to matter. Cars would move around other cars and run the lights. Pure chaos in the streets. But the energy of this city, I loved and I couldn't wait to explore. In the middle of the chaos was a huge Mall. A Mall bigger than any Mall I had seen in the States. It was called Sambil Mall. We pulled in a neighborhood that had beautiful gated buildings right on a side street off of the main street. We pulled up to a beautiful building that would be my residence. It had armed security outside of the first gate, a security booth at the next gate, a key fob entry Front door, key fob entry elevator and a key fob entry door to get to the hall where my apartment was. This was a highly secure building. And it should be because I was an American in a country that was hungry for money. There were rumors of Americans being kidnapped for ransom by hoodlums and cops. So they put us in a location where we could sleep safely and feel comfortable.

I dropped my bags as soon as I got in and was on my way to see the city. I soon learned that you were locked on my floor if you didn't have the key fob. It was secure and also kind of too secure, but I understood why. If you were visiting, you had to be walked all the way out the building, you couldn't enter nor exit without being assisted by a resident. I walked over to the main road in the direction of the mall I saw. It was about four blocks away from my apartment. Once I got to the mall, it was bigger than what I saw driving by it. The mall was called "Sambil Mall." This mall was amazing! It had everything in it. It was the biggest attraction in the city of Caracas

Venezuela. The streets were so busy and so much confusion. Anything could have been going on and you wouldn't know it. I didn't know Spanish at the time so I was a foreigner just filling my way through. I got a lot of attention because I was tall and American, so I was easily spotted and treated with a lot of smiles and verbal gestures that I couldn't understand.

Later that evening, a car picked me up to take me to the offices of the team. The team was called Cocodrillos de Caracas. At the office few people spoke English, every- one spoke Spanish. In these countries, their are differ- ent dialects of Spanish. Similar to slang. I thought it would be easier for me to learn Spanish than for them to learn english since I was the minority. A few of my teammates were there and they could speak a little bro- ken English that they've learned from other Americans that have played on the team previously. That helped a little, I needed them for translation until I could learn for myself. The guys were cool and funny. They cracked jokes all day, I knew that because they were always laughing and you could tell by their emotions. They all carried guns, which everyone did in that city who were not amongst the poor. Then I found out that my driver was my personal driver and was on call for me at any- time. I didn't take advantage of that because sometimes when i'm ready to make a move, I wanted to just leave, I didn't feel like waiting around for him. When we left the office, he took me for a drive around the city to see the sites and I wanted to see where the finer restaurants were and the nice places where the rich people would go to hang out. I came to find out that those places were right in my neighborhood. Caracas was a rich and poor city. It didn't have a middle class. The closest thing to middle class were the everyday workers that served the city. They didn't make a lot of money and lived in the ru- ins and ghettos.

My first day of practice was fun. My coach was an older guy who was big on fundamentals and drills. He re- minded me of The San Antonio Spurs coach Popovich. His practices were strictly fundamental and he was laid back and cool. He could speak a little English so that made my transition Smooth. Contrary to popular belief, I loved my coaches. I always wanted to be close to them, learn from them and pick them for all the knowledge that I could get. I wanted to be their friend. I wanted to be the guy they call to talk basketball too. I wanted them to be able to ask my opinion and feel comfortable doing it. But in some places, that was a gift and a curse. In the states, agents lean on coaches and what I mean by lean is, put pressure on coaches to play the players they rep- resent. I didn't have a agent. I didn't know who to trust. I didn't know who was true and who had my best inter- est. I didn't know who was really trying to help me. But my love for the game and to play overcame all of that. Because I was trying to kill all stereotypes and perceptions of me, it was easy for a coach to not put me out front and feature me. The guys who were the head cases and talked back, seemed to be the winners when it came to exposure. They would be the guys promoted to the scouts and the plays would be ran for, it was there team.

That issue was more state side. Internationally, they would send you home and bring another player in with no problem. But this coach really liked me. I didn't come to the team with and ego because I was an American and I was the best player, I just came to play ball and en- joy the experiences. As game day came around, I was so excited to see the fans and what the crowd was going to look like. The arena looked like one of the Stadiums in the movie 300. It was a tanned, stone outdoor arena. No roof and had a wood floor. It never rained on a game day and I was happy about that. That's one of the worst things to have a game cancelled. I want to play. I woke up on my first game day and tried not to eat much. I didn't want anything that would bother my stomach or could possibly slow me down. My driver arrived and I hopped in the car and felt the excitement of the day. The arena was like a 20 minute drive through the chaos and traffic. We were about five minutes out from the gym when a car pulled up beside us with guns drawn and pointing out the window at my car. My face dropped and fear came over me. My first thought was I have a game. In a weird way My thoughts were why this couldn't happen after the game. For a split second I thought I was about to get robbed. I looked in the car to see it was two of my teammates on the way to the arena. They were natives and started laughing and in broken English, they screened, "you scary, you scary!" They laughed as if it was the funniest thing in their lives. I couldn't believe these guys. What did they think? This isn't the normal in the states. We don't do random pull- ups on drivers with guns out. that happens, they're go- ing to shoot. After that interaction, they became our escorts and lead the rest of the way to the gym. Blowing their horns, running lights with both the driver and passenger heads and torsos out the window signaling people to move, I felt like royalty.

As we approached the arena, it was a big crowd outside early. It was like two hours before the game. The fans were there drinking beers, eating and it was like a standup tailgate party. We didn't have a special en- trance and had to walk through the crowd to get to the game. They knew the local players and greeted them normally. It wasn't the usual fan/player interaction that I was use to in the states, but so far my experience was great. My adrenaline was flowing, I was excited and I couldn't wait to play. When we entered the locker room, it was an old room with stone floors and lockers with fold out chairs. Our uniforms were already on a chair in front of our lockers. I sat and began to dump out my backpack and as I was taking out my things, all the local teammates were pulling their guns out of their waste belts. I was not use to this. When I took my sneakers out the bag, I was wearing Andɪ's at the time, they saw my sneakers and the conversation started. They wanted to know where I got the sneakers from and how could they get a pair. I hadn't been on tour yet, but I was endorsed by Andɪ. I told them I could get them some sneakers, and at that time Andɪ was looking out for me and would send the sneakers wherever I was. Sneakers were hard to get internationally especially places like Venezuela. The stores that did carry American sneakers had older models and they're were marked up higher than what they were in the states.

They asked did I know any Andɪ moves and I responded "No. I just hoop and whatever happens happens." I got dressed and went out to the floor to shoot around. It was sunny outside and hot but it was a great day for basket- ball. Being here in a new environment and having an opportunity to have a first impression and oppose my style of play on thousands of people, got me even more excited. While warming up, I was shooting deep shots and doing moves, playing one on one, I built up a good sweat and was actually ready for my second wind. The Gates opened and the fans started piling in and it didn't have ticketed seating because it was an open stone are- na. Remembering how the arena looked, and my love for the movie 300, I would watch the movie while I ate and got dressed fro the games. In my mind, I became the Marcus Arellius of Caracas. It wasn't hard to get into that role because that's what the arena looked like. I felt that way seeing all the people in the stadium looking down at me on the court. This first game was my first battle and I wanted to destroy my opponent and prove to the fans that I was the best player in this country. We returned to the locker room to get the game plan from our coach. It wasn't much of a plan because I was only able to participate in one practice. I was starting at Small Forward but had the freedom to create and was given ball handling responsibilities. Former Houston Rockets player Carl Herrera was on my team and was our starting Power Forward. He was a native and had just retired from the NBA.

As we returned back to the court, there was a live drum section in the stands and it was full to capacity. It was an amazing view and feeling. I had now switched to my Alter Ego and was ready to defeat and perform. The drums started playing another selection and the MC screamed something on the microphone in Spanish that I didn't understand, then the whole crowd got excited and started screaming. From under the tunnel behind me came a line of twenty of the most beautiful women I have seen in my life. They were the team dancers. The crowd started getting louder and the noise level was way up and this continued the entire game. I felt like I was at a international soccer game. The dancers lined up and their national anthem played and it was game time. We sat and the dancers created an alley for us to walk through when the starters were announced. My name was called last and I received a very loud welcome. The energy in this place was like nothing I had ever experienced before. It was the prime atmosphere to play and perform and entertain thousands of loyal fans. For two hours in a day they could escape the realities and the conditions they face everyday in their country. I could feel the release and the escape in the energy. I was ready to show out.

As the game begun, we were playing against a team that had a point guard that was really good. He was a Venezuelan local and a favorite of everyone. He could dribble and had moves. He was a floor general and a good shooter. He came out the gates firing. The game started off intense and physical. I was feeling my way through and getting my teammates involved. My thing was to create opportunities for other players because I knew I could get mine at any time. I could play a whole game and not worry about my numbers and have fun as long as we are winning. But if it's close, I want the ball in the final minutes. That's my time. I can win close games. In the first half, I began to get more involved because this guy on the opposing team was scoring left and right and he was putting on a show while doing it. I am so competitive, I play a game within the game. I played to not only win, but to out play my opponents. That was a deadly combination and not too many could figure out my why. I had a lot of back and forth competitions with- in a game against my opponents, but some forgot about winning. They would get caught up in the one on one and forget about why we're playing. This was another one.

Although we weren't guarding each other, I made it a personal competition with two words I said to him. I waited for the next play he converted, so that I could do the same thing he did, but do it better. Most guards were shorter than me so when they made a play that usually guards would only make, maybe a dribble move and fin- ish, I would do it at 6'8 and finish it with a dunk or a deeper three. He came down on this particular play in transition and hit one of our teammates with a cross- over then a spin move, he finished the play with a layup. I ran pass him and said "light work." He screamed at me in Spanish as if he understood and raised his head in the air and threw one of his hands up as to say, "get out of here." Same possession we go down court our and miss our shot, they get a fast break in transition and miss a jump shot, I got the rebound and started to push it up the sidelines, he ran towards me fast and I thought he was coming to foul me. He made a mistake and tried to cut the sidelines off and took a big step to get his foot on the line and I threw the ball between his legs. At that point right before he ran to me, i was already looking for an opportunity to make a play, and he brought it to me. When I got the ball after going between his legs, I did a spin just because that was how he scored on his last play. After that move, the crowd went crazy! It seemed like the players on both teams forgot about the game and stood still. I drove to the middle lane and it was clear and wide open, I threw the ball off the backboard caught it in the air and dunked it with one hand. This was a professional game and my teammates went crazy. They were jumping around like we won the Championship.

The coach on the other team called a timeout. I couldn't say that I got a standing ovation, because the fans were standing the whole time, the cheers I was receiving from the fans, made me want to take a bow. That one play, jump started my career in Venezuela. I became a favorite in Caracas. As the game continued, I was in the flow and entertaining. I had a good team of veterans that could play and score and similar my other teams, all i had to do was make sure we win and do the things necessary to do that. And one of those things was entertain. When I payed and entertained, It actually created a environment that felt good. Players were confident and relaxed and had fun. When you have this ingredients, you can play your best. I brought out everything in my arsenal, the fancy passes, the dribble moves the tricks and anything that I could create to entertain this crowd. On top of that, I was also putting up big numbers. I was quickly becoming one of the top players in the league.

The word started getting around the league fast about this player in Caracas who was me. My fan base started growing and fans in other cites would be waiting for our bus to pull up so they could see me. I was use to this treatment because it happened in every league that I played in around the globe. My style of play would al- ways make me a favorite and I knew that. Growing up in DC and playing summer league basketball, DC's Finest women would come to the games and the areas richest hustlers would be there as well and the girls wanted the best hoopers and the hostlers wanted the best hoopers to hang with them, so performing for the crowd was the norm. Getting the attention was the norm, but being in a third world country was different. The fans would stand outside the bus with little security. They wanted auto- graphs, they would touch you and this was during the walk to the arena. Some cities loved me and some hated me because they wanted to win.

Some cities would have a section that would cheer for me during our road games. In other cities, players would physically try to beat me down by any means. I played to win all fans over. My team and the opposing teams fans and I played better on the road than I did in home games. At home it's easier for everyone to play good be- cause you had the home crowd on your side. I would make sure everyone got their shine and that we won the game. I never played for numbers or stats, I could make plays whenever. I just played to win and did whatever was needed to do that. On the road it was adversity and I felt it was me against the world. My drive and motivation was in tact every game, I always felt that I had to prove myself. We were playing in Maracaibo and they had a older player who was a legend and one of the all time scorers in the league. he was much older than I was and looked a little out of shape. I guess folks were expecting me to pay homage to him because he was an old- er legend, but i went at him even harder. It was a close game and on one play, he punched me in the groin. I retaliated and pushed him and was thrown out the game immediately. No warning or anything. It was pretty much how the games went.

I didn't stop the way that I played, I continued to play my style, but i ended up with so many bruises and a cut over my eye that I got in a game from an elbow. It, didn't slow me down, I t made me go harder. By the halfway point, i was the best player i the league and in Caracas, I was treated like an Icon. Everywhere I went they knew me and I was amazed.

Caracas had two teams in the same town, Cocodrilos (my team) and the Panteras. The Panteras had three players from New York that I knew and one of them was a soon to be teammate named Lloyd Daniels that I would play with in Baltimore later in my career. I had known Lloyd from watching him play ball in New York and for the San Antonio Spurs. He was one of my favorite players. Lloyd was an older vet that was still a good player and he could shoot the ball. When we played the Panteras, It was a rival game, we were in the same city and the fans were divided. The first time we played them, we played at our home. As the game was starting, a couple of the Panteras fans were being escorted out. A young lady and a young man was walking out near the top of

the arena and as they passed the fans, they were getting beer thrown and poured on them until they exited the arena. We were standing there watching as it happened and the game was held until they were out. That had me hyped and ready to play. The Panteras had a really good team. They were in first place and I was ready for war. The game was a back and forth game and I got to see Loyd play up close and in personal. He wasn't fast or athletic, but he could get his shot off with anybody in his face and make it. While playing against him, I was studying his game. He was an amazing passer also and had a high IQ. I was amazed at his skill set and how he played such a high level game at a Smooth and laid back pace. I played fast and was one of the best in transition, but watching Lloyd, i had to add his style to my game. So I did.

During that game, when we were in a half court setting, I started copying Lloyd in the game. To some that's not the time to be trying new things, but that was the base of my development. If i liked it, i added it to my game. What I liked the most was his style of triple threat. He didn't do the conventional or fundamental triple threat, he stood straight up in a position where he had an ad- vantage because of his size and he could see over the defense. But the way he stood, he could shoot in one motion, pass in one motion or jab. He also could lean in to your body and without dribbling shoot a fadeaway. I hadn't seen this arsenal before and now it was mine. He could tell I was copying because he said to me after one play, "I see you young fella." I had gotten better in the middle of a game watching Lloyd Daniels.

We won the first game against the Panteras and then lost the second one at their home. After the second game was when I knew the effect I had on this city. During the city in a one month span, I played with seven different Americans. If you didn't perform, if we lost or if you were hurt or injured and couldn't give 100%, you were shipped out and shipped out fast. after a bad game, the next game it would be two new Americans on the bench in street clothes just arriving from the airport. It was strategic and intentional and I thought it was to push the three Americans to see who will perform the best to stay and the other two will be shipped out. I wasn't worried because I was performing at a high level and I was the most popular player in the league. When we played the Panteras at their arena, I was having a great game and made my first three three's to start the game. Then on my next shot, similar to my incident in Philadelphia, the defender ran underneath me and I landed on his foot. I didn't turn my ankle nor injure my achilles, but the two bones in the front of my leg where the femur is, had a surge of pressure shoot up between them and pushed the bones apart. They didn't break or dislocate, they took on a curved like shape as a a horse- shoe. I've never heard of this and didn't know until I got an X-ray. I went to the bench with this unusual pain thinking it would go away and I would be able to continue. This is a big game. Our rivals, first place and in the sam city. The coaches and the GM kept coming to me to see if I was ready and I tried to go back out there and I couldn't run. I came out the game and the looks on everyones face were of disgust. My days were numbered and I knew i was going home.

To my surprise, after the game they took me to the hospital. Their hospital was different from ours and I was very uncomfortable there. I wouldn't allow them to give me anything or take any needles. The only thing they could do is touch it and try and figure it out. They said it was a sprain and I could continue in a week. They let me stay the whole week and rest and even got treatment for me everyday. I got massages and acupuncture for the first time. They wanted to wait it out and see if I would get better and could play again. After the week was up, I attended practice and tried to play through the little minor pain and discomfort I still had. Then while doing sprints, I felt a sharp pain and went to sit down. I told them I would ice and play the next day. When game time approached, I got treatment before the game and got my leg taped. The tape was uncomfortable, but I wanted to play. I started the game and from the start, I couldn't do it. I really thought I would be sent home by then, but no. They gave me another week. After that week I still hadn't gotten better. I got a call to come to the office to see the GM. She was a tall woman that looked like a Boss. She didn't smile much but would when i began to learn Spanish and she would laugh when I slipped over words, but she loved that I was really trying. She greet- ed me as soon as I came in and we walked to her office and we sat. She handed me my check and I thought a plane ticket was next, but what she said next, shocked me because I have seen so many Americans in and out the door. She asked me did I know of anyone who could come and take my place while I got healthy. I was shocked!! Did she just ask me to fly a friend in to play in my place while I got healthy? Wow! This had to be a first. I had just left playing in Tampa and I wanted to win this league and she felt we had a chance to win it all with me, so I called up Ace Custis. Ace was on my team in Tampa and he was having a really good season. Ace was my first choice. Ace came to town and they moved him in the apartment right next door to me. I couldn't believe that this just happened.

Another week went by and games were played, then I was sent to get a X-ray. It was then that I saw what was wrong and i had to stay off my leg to allow it to fully re- cover. I ended up staying in Caracas for a full month, got paid and didn't play a game after a injury. That's how much the team liked me. She asked if I wanted to go home and get that taken care of because I wasn't comfortable with their doctors. I finally left and returned home. Cocodrilos de Caracas took care of me and was one of the best experiences of my life. As all good things come to an end, so did this one. I truly could have stayed in Caracas forever and built a career there. But when i returned home, I got right back in to the American Leagues and planned to return to Venezuela the following summer. .

Chapter XIX:

THE NETS

UPON MY RETURN home and after my leg had healed, was when I became the King of the next few summers at Rucker Park. I was playing for Murder Inc. at the time. My guy Todd who i will introduce in the Rucker Chapter, helped me move on to a New team from Black Hand. I was a free agent and had a lot of interest from all over the city. I landed with Murder Inc. Irv Gotti, Chris Gotti and Ja Rule. The Inc. as they are now called after some legal issues, were the hottest label at the time. Ja Rule, Ashanti were topping the charts, Charlie Baltimore was killing the streets and my DC homie Chink Santana was the hottest producer along with producer Jimi Hendrix. Murder Inc. were free agents at the time and were hav- ing meetings with the top record execs. One of the execs that they were holding meetings with, was also a part owner of the New Jersey Nets. Irv, Chris and I had

talked about my career and they wanted to understand why I wasn't in the NBA. They have seen me play numerous times against other NBA players and and also talked to a few players about me including Kobe Bryant. Kobe told Chris Gotti and the CEO of Translation, a marketing agency, that he wants me in L.A. So in our conversation, I mentioned to them that I was a victim of the politics. I had a few agents that wouldn't tell me the truth but one told me I was in he middle of some politics that he couldn't change. I could get work outs at this time, but i could never get a fair eye. I always went in situations where the odds were doubled down against me. So Irv said I can get around that. He asked the own- er who was interested in his label if he could get me a fair eye, and I would handle the rest. He told him to trust me, this guy will handle his business. he just needs a fair eye. Irv words got through and it worked.

I was back home at Barry Farms playing in a game and we were up twenty points so I went and sat on the bench. While I was sitting on the bench, my phone rang. This was an outdoor league and anything goes, so I looked at my phone. It was a number i didn't recognize. Back then I answered all out of state calls because most likely it was for basketball. I answered the phone and as I thought, it was for basketball. a voice as I answered said, "Lonnie?" I returned, "this is he." He said, "this is Rod Thorn of the New Jersey Nets." It was loud with the music playing and the game was going on. So I jumped up and said, "hold on for one second please." I sprinted off the court and ran up to the next block when i couldn't hear any noise from the court. Rod asked are you at a game, I told him I was playing, but i just ran a block away so I can hear. he started laughing and said Lonnie can you come to New Jersey tomorrow? I told him I sure can. He said go ahead and play your game and my assistant will call you tonight to schedule and get you up here. I was so excited. Irv got me what I wanted!

The Nets had spots available on their team. They just traded for Jason Kidd that summer and Kerry Kittles was injured. So I felt this would be a great opportunity for me. I went back to the court and told my friend Lavelle who was coaching us at the time about the call. He said I knew it was something how you ran out of here so fast. I didn't play the rest of the game so I wouldn't get hurt. I got the call to arrange my travel for the next day to arrive in New Jersey. I was excited and began to prepare myself mentally for this trip. I laid down and just thought about my workouts. I've been to so many and I knew what to expect, but this time felt like this was the one i need. I'm in the politics and i will get a fair eye. I was ready to go. I thought about the drills and how I will move quick and not fast so I can show my footwork and get into my shots. I thought about defense and how I will be deceptive to get by players and make them look like they didn't have a chance to guard me. I was so confident in my skill set and I was actually the best that I had ever been at that time of my career. I was dangerous! I thought about playing five on five, running the lanes, de- fending and showing all facets of my game and figuring out how I can fit and make sure to ask the coaches how do you see me fit. When i arrived, i got to the hotel and they had an itinerary for me at the front desk. I went to the gym that evening and met the coaches after they had just finished up practice with their summer league team. I caught the end of the practice and saw a few familiar faces from other leagues that i had played in be- fore. I went to dinner and then returned to my hotel to pray and then channel my focus on my workout. The next morning after breakfast, I headed to the gym for my workout. I was the only one there. Usually it's a few other players there together working out but I was the alone player. Head Coach Byron Scott, assistance Eddie Jordan and Lawrence Frank were there to hold the workout. The GM Rod Thorn walked in later and sat by the door to watch the workout. The workout consisted of a lot of shooting and running. I was locked in and made it through the workout with no problems. I was in shape' felt good and I made sure they knew that. So after the workout, Coach B, or Coach Scott as he was called, said good job, i'll be in touch with you soon. I knew that I wasn't going to find out anything that day, so I felt good when i left because of how I got invited to the workout was through Irv's relationship with one of the owners. I went to eat and returned to my room for the night and packed to go home in the morning.

I got a phone call from Rod Thorn that night in my room. He asked could I come back for another workout in the morning and that the room would be taken care of for another day. I quickly said yes and thanks. So the next morning I go to the workout and completed it, and then Coach B asked me to stay and practice with the summer league team coming in. Did they think I was go- ing to turn them down? I responded well of Course I will. Thank God I was in the best shape ever because I was putting everything out in my workout. Now it was what I was expecting, playing against other players. The practice was more drills than anything. Like a group workout and a lot of shooting drills. We did half court shell drills and the was the most team stuff we did. We didn't get to play. That was alright with me because I had a hard workout before the practice. After practice Coach B said I want you to come back tomorrow. This was day number three. So I followed my same routine. I was here for business so i wasn't going into the city (New York), as tempted as I was to go. After practice I took an ice bath and got a massage from the trainer, then i went to eat and returned to my room. The next day when i arrived to the gym, i had a practice uniform with my name on it and one of the players who was there the day before, was gone. One of my the guys I met name was Mark Sanford. Mark was an athletic slasher that could finish and shoot. He and I became buddies during our time there and became long term friends after we left. Mark was a funny guy and made a joke about me taking someones spot in a day.

That day we scrimmaged. Man if teams determined who was on the team from actually playing, I would have made every NBA team i tried out for. This time I had a chance. I balled out! I had the coaches and the players in awe of my game and how I shot the ball. Practice was good for me. I spoke with coach Eddie Jordan after practice who was also a Washingtonian representing D.C. and he cracked a joke about my shooting. I told him if I take ten three pointers in a game, i'm going to make seven. he looked at me and said, it's not going to be this easy in Boston. I looked and was thinking, what's in Boston? But before i could ask any questions, he said we want you to play on our summer league team that goes to Boston next week. I held my composure but in my soul I was shouting and screaming yes, yes, yes!!! I stayed calm and told him thanks and he pointed me to the training room where I was to sign my contract and i didn't return back to D.C. Yes I was there for one day for a workout that ended in a summer job. I went and bought me some clothes and I was in new Jersey for daily practices until it was time to go.

A few days after that, we went to scrimmage the New York Knicks. I didn't play a lot but when I got in, I made a few shots. Rick Brunson was playing for the Knicks and he started guarding me after a few of my shots and he said, i know who you are, i'm not letting you shoot. Rick and I use to hoop together with Allen Iverson and Dejuan Wagner playing two on two at Temple. He knew I could shoot the ball but the other players didn't really pay me that much attention because I entered the game late in the first half. They didn't know I was as good as the players who started, but I had just walked on the team. So my time was limited. Richard Jefferson, Brian Scalabrine, Brandon Armstrong and Jason Collins were drafted rookies and the stars of the summer. So i was pretty much fighting for minutes for one spot, that's how it works. Summer league is for the drafted rookies and maybe one or two more free agents. Everyone else are filling out the team for practice numbers so there is enough to simulate game situations. But I wasn't there for that, not in my mind anyway, i was there to make the team. I played solid in the scrimmage and now it was time to head to Boston.

I was excited to go to Boston, it was the home of my college and where some of my best friends live that I met in college. I hooked up with my friends as soon as I got to town, we had enough time to grab a bite to eat and I got back to the room before curfew. A lot of my friends and school mates came out to support me. I got decent time in summer league but i didn't get a lot of time. I got a few shots here and there and mostly ran the point. I remember the game against the 76ers and Speedy Claxton was guarding me. Everyone know how fast and quick Speedy was. Speedy had a good NBA career and was a good player. It was another player that i knew on the Sixers that also played in Boston at Boston University who I use to clash with in college, Roger Bell. Roger was a really good defender and best known for guarding Kobe in the playoffs and their dislike for each other was on the stage in the playoffs when Roger played in Phoenix later in his career. Speedy was guarding since i was playing the point and he was pushing up like a ton of others because i was tall and i guess I looked like I can't dribble. Also because my playing time was sporadic, they thought i was a bench player or couldn't play or something. He was reaching and I was just getting to my spots and running the offense. i didn't get any shots because by the time I started the offense, the ball never came back and I wasn't one of the players that was drafted that could just go and hoop. i was trying to make the team. Speedy made me start trash talking to him because I had to let him know that i was official and he never ripped me or stole the ball. But i got smart and figured out an offense I could call and pass and cut to the block and call for it back, and turned and shot over him a couple times. I found a way to manipulate the offense. The Nets ran a variation of the triangle offense, it wasn't any set plays unless you were calling something specific for a certain player, but I didn't have to call any- thing for anyone. Most of the time I was in the game with Brandon Armstrong who was also a cool guy that had become a friend. He would pass me the ball as I got more playing time so i could get shots. He was a scorer and everyone knew he could score but he was very un- selfish and wasn't playing to make the team. He was al- ready on it. Our biggest game and it was the most hyped game was against the Washington Wizards and Michael Jordans first number one draft pick, Kwame Brown. Now all the hype was around Kwame Brown and after seeing him play, rightfully so. Yes I said rightfully so. Kwame was a big and skilled athlete and he didn't have a number one pick career, but it's more to it than he be- ing a bust. This game was on ESPN and it was sold out! I wasn't expecting to play at all this game and my number got called early. I loved the the big lights and i was ex- cited when Coach B said, "Ledge." he called Me Ledge, short for Lonnie legend. That was the name he gave me. I got another nickname to add to the list. I went to the scorers table and the atmosphere was crazy! My Boston friends and fans cheered when I entered the game. I had more support than I expected. Fans from College came out to cheer me on. I started playing more towards the end of the summer and this game was towards the end. By this time I knew how to manipulate the offense to get the ball back. In the triangle, the passers cut let every- one know what to do next. I passed it to the wing, then cut down to the block, a few games ago, I would post up when i had a smaller guard, this time I would wait for the ball to be reversed and then get a down screen and pop to the top for above the three point line. The top of the key was my spot, I could take that three with my eyes closed. I did that four times through out the game. I went 3-4 from the three point line. I had a really good game and played long enough to get some comfortable shots up. A friend of mine recorded the game and sent me a clip of a comment the commentator made after one of my made shot's. "Who is this Harrell kid? He can play and really shoot the ball." It's always good to hear those kind of comments, but the goal is to make the team.

I had a good summer with the Nets and before I re- turned home, Coach B told me he was going to invite me back for Veterans camp. I was excited to hear that and when I got home, it was on! Time to get stronger and in even better shape. My regimen at the time was simple. I would run on the elliptical, jump rope, do pull-ups and play ball. My workout would be more mental than physical. I would make 500 shots and 50 free throws. I didn't like to shoot stand still or set shots. I had to be moving. I knew what the game felt like, so I recreated the foot- work, speed and timing when I shot so the game would never be too fast for me. Playing pickup was the best preparation for me. i could control my speed and pace and play the game in my head. It also helps with your timing and conditioning. When it was Tim to show up to camp, I was ready and in shape. When you're taking the route I took, you're always treated like a rookie. One of my requirements was to arrive at the gym early. I had to get my ankles taped first, and then start working out be- fore practice started. That's a part of your test. You have to work harder than anyone to prove that you wanted it and they were going to make sure that you worked.

The practice experience in New Jersey was different than the other camps I went too. Coach B had us doing a lot of running. We started practice off with fifteen minutes on the clock and we had to run backwards laps for the whole fifteen minutes. We did sprints and this is where I saw how Kenyon Martin was a different athlete. He was in the line with the guards and would beat all of us including Jason Kidd and finish his last sprint back- wards, while we had one more. He was a different type of athlete. While working out before our second practice was to begin, i was off to the side with Coach Frank. I was so locked in, I blacked out and didn't remember the work out. We were doing two practices a day (called two a days) during training camp. The first practice was conditioning and a lot of learning. The second practice was a team scrimmage. Coach B walked over to me after working out with Coach Frank, he said Ledge, I heard you didn't miss a shot in your workout? I was sweating and breathing hard and told him, "I don't remember". I was so locked in and ready to play. I was on the team with Jason Kidd and played really well. Jason had given me a compliment by saying that I could push the ball and it made transition easier for him. But that day, i continued making all my shots. I was on fire! My last shot of the scrimmage, I was running for a loose ball, I jumped out of bounds behind the basket about 7 feet from the rim on the baseline, I turned to look for someone to throw it to, and no one was open. In mid air, I shot the ball over the backboard and it went in. Coach B blew the whistle for a long time and said, "that's it! We're done!" He turned to me and said, "got damn!" Practice ended and my shoot- ing black out continued through the scrimmage.

As training camp came to a close, it was the eve before our first pre-season game. We were in practice shooting around, then the team trainer came and asked me to come in the training room. He told me that the Doctor wanted to review something from my physical. I asked him "what did he want to review?" He said he wanted to run some test on your heart. My mood immediately changed and my heart dropped and my stomach started turning. Here I was having a great camp and I strongly believed that I earned a spot on this team and now this. They took me straight to the hospital and the Doctor saw me as soon as I got there.

I walked in the Doctors office and they wasted no time in seeing me. I immediately had to change in to work out clothing and the nurses put white patches all over my body from head to toe. Then she attached wires to all of the patches and then injected ink into my system. The ink was so they could get a Clear projection of my heart while it worked. After I was hooked to the wires, i felt like the bionic man, i got on a treadmill and they connected the wires to a machine. I ran on the treadmill for 30 minutes. After that, I was laid on a table and they were running test on me. It was the most frustrating thing that i have experienced. I am not a fan of hospitals as I guess that no one is, but this whole situation raised my stress levels. I was thinking about so much and so many things the whole time I was running. My sweat was hiding my tears from my frustration, but I was alone in the room as I ran. The nurse would come in to check the machine and make sure none of the cords came out. After the testing was over, I had been in the hospital having test run for over two hours. I went back to my room and could not eat and called my Mother. I cried while talking to my mother like a little boy. I was devastated and I was broken because I knew that nothing good would come from this. As always, she prays and says that "God got it. Keep your faith in God and his will, will be done." I believe that and always whatever the outcome is, It's his divine plan and I move on to what's next. She always sooth me and calm my nerves and I'm able to sleep when I talk to her. She has been through this every step of the way without having an opinion. She trust that I will make good decisions and she prays for me. That's all i could ask for from her and she has been on this ride with from start to finish.

The next Morning, Coach B called me to his office before practice began. He said, "Legend, you were having a great camp. Unfortunately Thorn (the GM) is afraid to keep you because of your condition. The Doctor said you have an enlarged heart and a heart murmur, similar to what Reggie Lewis had and he doesn't want to risk that. If it was up to me and i was the decision maker, I would keep you." I had to keep my face together and just said thank you and kept it short. He said "I haven't seen many shoot the ball like that, keep shooting." I turned and walked out the door. I went back in the gym to say my goodbye's to the guys i grew close too, and the was the last time I would be a part of an NBA team.

Chapter XX:
NBDL
(G-League)

A FEW WEEKS after being in New Jersey, I got a call to attend the Inaugural Draft Camp of the National Basket- ball Developmental League. It was the NBA's farm league called the D-League at the time. Today it's called the G-League because Gatorade is the title sponsor of the league. It was kind of funny to me that I couldn't play in the NBA because of my heart review, but i could play in their farm league. Can't die upstairs, but i can down stairs. This time I went to Georgetown (my former School) and got my physical from the school Doctor. He said that my readings were similar to my readings in College. It made me think. I didn't have any proof and I couldn't prove it, but athletes have something called an athletic heart. Most have heart murmurs and it's normal. My thoughts were that I performed so good in camp, the connections that got me the original workout were strong, and they couldn't cut me because of performance and this was another way to do it. It only makes since because i shouldn't have played in the D- League if that was the case.

I flew to North Carolina for this D-League pre-draft camp. I just came from the Nets camp with a Chip on my shoulder and I was ready to go at every player that got in front of me. During the check in, I had a hoodie on and I didn't speak to anyone. I went through the lines, got the information that was needed and went to my room and relaxed until it was time to play. The pre-draft camp was for NBA prospects to play in front of the scouts from all 32 NBA teams in tournament style games to be evaluated and for the D-League GM's and Coaches to evaluate for the draft. Similar to the NFL combine except we just played ball. I saw a familiar face that I knew from the Rucker in New York named Booger Smith. Booger was playing in the game before mine, so i watched his game to support him. I played in my very first game at Rucker Park against Booger and his team Soul In The Hole. We were up next. My first game I showed off and really was out there just showing off be- cause at this point, i felt I was chasing a ghost but played because I loved the game. I didn't have any pressure on me to perform and I treated the games like summer league game and was having fun. Other players who were there came to our court and watched me show off. After I finished playing, I was taken in a back room for a photo shoot with a journalist from ESPN. They did a feature story on myself and Rashad Phillips from Detroit. Rashad was killing at the camp and we were the two most exciting players there. We both were drafted in the top 10 and of the 100 players there, I was the second oldest player in the camp. Most of the guys were one and two years out of college. I was the tenth pick in the draft; NBDL Inaugural Draft 2001. These are the first ten picks of the draft.

#1 Chris Andersen, #2 Terrance Roberson, #3 Rahim Lockhart, #4 Gabe Muoneke, #5 Johnny Hemsley, #6 Neil Edwards, #7 Rashad Phillips, #8 Artie Griffin, #9 Darrell Johns, #10 Lonnie Harrell

After being selected in the draft by the Huntsville Flight, we got feed back and evaluations from the scouts and coaches that were present. The evaluations came from the coaches and other media guys around. The things I heard about myself, made me laugh. They were more excuses and ifs than actual things or should I say facts. One scout said "he can do everything, but I'm not sure how he would do against the guys in the league." It took me back to the comment Rick Barry made about me when he said, " He's a great player, I would like to see how he plays against Scottie Pippen." I felt Rick Barry's was a compliment, and this one was an excuse to not calling me up. I have competed against the NBA's best over the past years and that comment sounded like he was just saying anything to give an answer. It's only one way to find out, and that's by being given a chance instead of wondering what if. But that was something out of my control. I had to just do what i could control, and that's play ball.

We traveled back to our individual homes after the camp. We had a couple of weeks before we had to report to our teams. Huntsville, Alabama was where my team was located. The only thing I could think of was that Alabama was racist and full of country folk. While I was at home, I continued my workout regimen, to get in the best shape possible. What my Coach at Georgetown said to me, stuck with me throughout my entire career;

"They can't push what they can't catch."

I got in tip top shape and fatigue was never an issue. As long as I could run forever, I couldn't be guarded. I showed up in Huntsville for another training camp. I had just left New Jersey maybe a month before, now i'm here having to go through another camp. This camp was more mental in that, I didn't want to go through it again, but I was on a team with new players and coaches, so I had to prove myself again. The first day of camp, I had to win the sprints, I had to jump the line and get extra reps, be- cause it seemed some of the players already knew the coaches. I didn't know anyone. Quickly it was clear that favoritism was going on. I was the most skilled player on the team but no matter what I did, the coach had his favorites. I was use to earning mine in practice so i wasn't worried. Also I knew I would get that chance in a game when someone was in foul trouble or an injury, and I would play the bulk of the minutes. It's a part of the game and i was always ready for my moment.

It would take about four games before I was a starter. I didn't look back after that. The games were fun and it was a lot of good players that would move on to the have NBA careers from this league. As usual, I would have my bumps in the road. The first year I would have a good season. The team was solid and in leagues like this, teams will have a lot of scorers. We had six players averaging double figures and the leading scorer was Terrence Roberson from Saginaw, Michigan. he played at Fresno State and averaged thirteen points a game. He only played fourteen out of the 56 games. Myself and Snap Hunter took over after he left. Snap was probably my best and most fun backcourts mate ever. We both played the same style game. Fast paced, athletic play- makers. We had great chemistry and talked trash to each other during the game. That's how we used to hype each other up. I would ask him what you going to do? I expected him to tell me how he was going to do his opponents. We challenged each other in practice and in the games. Having a player I could relate to on and off the court made playing on this team better. Snap was from Memphis Tennessee. He attended Memphis University before transferring to Life College. At both. Memphis and Life, he was the leading scorer. He didn't drop off when he came to Huntsville. Neither of us got a call up our first year and we were two of the most talented and exciting players in the league.

My second year was when I started really seeing the politics in the league. After year one, I came back on a mission. I was at my best ever. I had a great preseason and I let it be known in camp that this was my year. I got stronger and was in tip top condition as always. With my new strength, I started to defend better and rebound more. I lead my team in three statistical categories through the first ten games, until one road game I will never forget. I was the talk of the league an i felt i couldn't be denied this season, a call up to the league. We played on the road and I get excited when I want others to see the progress. I played my best games on the road because most players play better at home, so the road was mine. I was a road warrior. We were play- ing against the leagues leading scorer the year before and I couldn't wait to get at him. Also on that team was another player who got called up and had a really good NBA career. They were mine. The player who lead the league in scoring was a post player and the other guy was a wing defender. Wasn't to great offensively, but he was a hard nosed defender. I came out fast right after jump ball. I had six points and seven rebounds in the first quarter. I felt different, I was ready to dominate the game. I thought if any year I would prove that I was different from the other players, It was this year. The second quarter began and I was still on. My numbers had leaped to thirteen points and ten rebounds and five assist, with time left in the quarter. Then after getting my 11th rebound, a player took my legs out in the air and i landed on one leg with my knee in a locked position and had the worst pain and feeling on the side of my knee ever. I was punching the floor and screaming, but the screaming was anger. Here we go again. Every time I think I have the best opportunity, something would happen. My teammates stand me up and with assistance, I hobbled to the training room. I'm thinking it's over. After sitting in the locker room the whole half icing, the pain calmed and it was tolerable. I stood up to see how it felt with putting pressure on it, and I could tolerate the pain. No X-ray or anything, I returned to the game. I couldn't fully move like I was before I went down, because i still had a pain in my knee and I didn't know what it was. I felt I had to play because I started the season so great and didn't want a set back. I could still play at a high level, but i wasn't flying around and going for rebounds like I was before.

I was still able to lead my team in scoring that season. My rebounds and assist had dropped and so did other statistical categories, but i was still the same competitor and getting it done. We had a break for a week and I would go to Atlanta to hang out with some family and friends. One evening I was at dinner at Justin's the restaurant the was owned by Diddy. It was the spot to be. All of ATL's industry execs, artist and taste makers hung out there. I was at the bar having a drink and making my rounds acknowledging friends before we sat. I saw a NBA exec there that i know. He was alone at the bar, so I went over to speak to him and he told me this story. He said, "man, we called your team to call you up." I asked "so what's the hold up?" He told me the coach said; "you should take this other player. He's a pro and he played on an NBA team already.

He's a vet, a leader and he would be a better fit. He has a better work ethic and has a family." When I heard that, I completely shut off. The room stopped, I couldn't hear the DJ play- ing the popular songs of that area that helped created this sexy crowd. And he could see it on my face. I was waiting for him to say something to make me feel better and not drive back down the road and knock on the coaches apartment door. He just stood there with me, and without saying anything, I felt he was thinking the same and was encouraging me to go and do that with the smirk on his face. I was so pissed. It was hard for me to enjoy myself for the next few days in Atlanta with that on my mind, but at that time, Atlanta was the place to be and it totally eased my mind and showed me what really matters, my mental health and my life. I was in a great place to find that type of news out. I was around people who supported me and genuinely loved me for who i was and not just because I played basketball. They liked Lonnie the fun guy, the charismatic guy who got along with everyone and made new friends in every room he walked in. That's who i was and that's who i remained.

When i went back to Huntsville, I practiced as if nothing had happened. I worked hard, i competed in games, and the guy the exec mentioned, got called up to that team. Unfortunately for me, the NBA Coach and GM makes that decision, the guy I knew, wasn't the one who could make that happen. He did his part and also gave me in- formation he didn't have to give. I would have never known what was going on, if he hadn't told me. The thing that connected the dots, was that the coach and the guy in mention, use to go out and drink beers together. I could see that conversation transpiring over a beer and becoming fond of each other. With that information in the back of my head, my approach to the game really came into focus, and everything became about me and what I wanted. I spent years trying to avoid the rumors and stereotypes I heard about myself, and the area i was raised in. In doing so I was afraid to be myself on and off the court. That changed. I was never a headache and always coachable, but now the filter had fallen off so i did whatever i felt was right for me. Now if I was hurt or injured, I wasn't going to practice and push through it. I was going to care for my body since no one else did. I sacrificed and played on an injured knee and ankle, because I didn't want to miss an opportunity and show my durability. I couldn't make those sacrifices anymore because it wasn't appreciated. it wasn't worth it. The NBA dream was to play on the biggest level of basketball and show the world how i would have developed on that level, with those resources. I wanted to go higher. I never thought about a contract or the money, I just wanted to show my game to the world.

One evening we were out eating and our coach was there as well. I got the opportunity to confront him when we got back to our apartments. I went with the vibes of the evening and allowed everyone to enjoy themselves, i caught a moment afterwards to approach him. I told him what i've heard and who i heard it from and he had no choice but to come clean. He was honest and repeated what I was told, that the player had kids, and was getting married and didn't have any money. He really needed the money. I told him that was foul and I couldn't respect hi anymore. Everyone has a situation and because you feel sorry for his, you take away an opportunity from someone else who deserved it? If they would have asked you to pick a player I get it. But they asked specifically for me and you sold them someone else. Needless to say he only lasted the ten days and he was back on the team. This time when he returned, he was on a mission. He started taking all the shots because he was in the league for ten days and felt entitled. It ruined the chemistry on our team, we started losing games and players started distancing themselves from each other. I still lead the team in scoring, but it was every man for himself.

The following season which was my third season in the league, It was a few new faces on the team. We had the same coach and by this time, the league started to strategically place players around the league. For this experience, now it was two guys who was getting all the attention in practice and taking all the shots. I was find with that because I always used practice to out compete and out perform whoever. This time was no different. I went hard in camp and I would get the rebound and go coast to coast and beat everybody down the floor in transition and lay the ball up. I would do it over and over and couldn't be stopped. By the time our first game approached, I was traded to Georgia to play for Jeff Malone. Jeff was a cool payers coach and he use to play for my hometown team the Washington Bullets. Jeff was a great scorer who's mid range was his strength. He was one of Michael Jordans best competitors. Jeff was hard on me because he felt that i should have been in the NBA. He told me that I wasn't there because of me and he was going to find out why. He pushed me but by this time, I was over chasing a ghost. Georgia was a tier low- er than Huntsville. I had built a fan base in Huntsville. We had the best attendance, I had a lot of fans who still reached out to me and emailed me years after I was gone. I gave the kids gear and accessories that Andı would send me and I participated in their community. Snoop even had a concert in our Arena and wore my Huntsville jersey on stage as he performed. Some have said I was the best player to play in Huntsville. I actually really liked being there. In Georgia, it was in a small town in the middle of nowhere. The practice floor was tile and your feet and legs would hurt during and after practice and it was about me and my health by the time I got there. The first few days of practice per the norm, I went at all my teammates. I had to let them know what I bring to the table. Then the team started losing me men- tally. I am a guy who pays attention to mental health. Studying psychology in college, i knew the things that could be stressful and ware you down in these type of environments and when i sensed them, I would remove myself from them. Jeff didn't like it, but that's what it was going to be. I would still compete hard in games, I never cheated the game. I gave my all from start to finish.

My time in Georgia would be shortened after one particular game. I went through the season starting and playing pretty well. We had a home game against a team from Virginia. As I was warming up, I saw a familiar face at the NBA scouts table behind the basket. It was the coach from the Atlantic City team in the USBL. He won the Championship in that league multiple times and had the better team each year. He recruited me every year and I wouldn't play for him. I was determined to beat him and i told him that. He saw me warming up and asked, "what are you doing here?' I responded, "I got traded here at he start of the season." He said, "no, i mean in this league? I saw you play, i know how you play, you shouldn't be here." I laughed and continued to listen to his rant. He said, "we get this list every week and it has players to watch and those are the players we can call up, and your name is not on here. I'm an Indiana Pacers scout and Reggie (Miller) went down and we need to bring someone up until he's well. I've seen you play. You should be on this list." After hearing that, that was it. It was the last straw. My mind was made up and I was done with the NBDL effective immediately.

I wanted to leave right then and not play the game, but it was two guys on the team from New York that I heard so much about and I wanted to play against them. I had even more motivation for this game. As soon as the game started, I was shooting. Every time I touched the ball i was shooting it. i didn't care. I had thirty points by the half and Jeff Malone was pissed because I rebelled and wouldn't pass the ball. He benched me the second half and I didn't play anymore. I was fine with that and I was finished with the NBDL. After the game, I went back to my apartment and started packing a bag. I was head- ed back to Miami. I bought a ticket that night and caught the last flight out. While at the airport, I called the President of the league. He answered the call and since it was after a game, he asked was everything ok. I proceeded to tell him my issues. I started with questions. Do you think I deserve to get a workout or a call up? I've been the best player on my team and others getting workouts and call ups and i'm not getting either. He responded with a very dry, "Yes. i think you do." So what's the problem? He didn't have an answer for me. I told him, I'm done. I'm at the airport now. I'm not play- ing anymore and thanks for the opportunity. He said, "you will get fined." I said you're not listening, you can have those checks, i won't play another game and i'm on my way home and hung up. My next call was to my teammates I was cool with. they were roommates and I called and told them I was at the airport, but I left my door unlocked and it's sneakers, sweats and all kinds of gear in the boxes in my room. Y'all can have it. My next call was to one of the execs at Andi. I told him, i'm leaving the D League, I'm coming on tour.

My pro experience, many wouldn't understand my early transition. I had a lot of tough games adjusting to how i was played. In most leagues, I played against double teams and I wasn't the primary player on most of my teams. That caused me to force things and figure things out for myself. Non NBA professional leagues are not like the NBA in detail and game planning. It's every man for himself. Everyone is trying to get called up to the NBA so you have to get in where you fit in. Most of these teams I started off on the bench and was able to work my way to the starting lineup through practice. This was every team I played for. But being so young and playing against every teams best defender with a lot of attention being paid to my offensive skill set, was a struggle for me and something I had to overcome alone without any guidance. I wasn't a volume shooter or scorer because I was never ushered in as a player. I had to try out and make every team I played on, so i'm play- ing a game within the game. The difference is like the experiences in AAU. People remove their kids from play- ing on a team where the coach has a kid on the team. That's the reality of the game on all levels. Players are treated differently and all players aren't equal. That's an early lesson that should be used to create that competitive hunger in a player and not remove yourself or run from it. At the end of the day, the cream will always rise to the top. Don't run from adversity on your way to your goals push through them. I fought against all the adversity thrown my way but it became a time in my mid thirties, that I had to face the music and start taking care of me. I am good with my decisions and blessed for the experiences I have had and the career opportunities I was awarded. I was truly blessed by God. I am very thankful.

"The only person you are destined to become is the person you decide to be." - Ralph Waldo Emerson

Chapter XXI:

DEVELOPMENT

My INTRODUCTION TO player development started once I was asked to train a friend's kids. I started out doing the things that I used to do with my college coaches during our individual workouts. Then I found that most of the kids couldn't do the things I was teaching, and it didn't benefit them from what I was seeing. I have never seen the kids play in games before, so I couldn't assess what's needed to help them in game play. So I would talk to the parents and get an idea of what they needed. As you could probably guess, most always say ball handling. What turned me away from focusing on ball handling with younger kids, was a situation I had with a 10 year old kid. My Cousin (I call him my nephew) Kevin Harrell and some of his friends were training with me at the time and they were pretty advanced for their age group. They were #1 in the Country at the time playing 10 and Under for AAU. They won the National AAU Championship at that age group. One of their friends was on the team and never got in the game. His parents switched teams to a team that didn't have as many talented players, so he could get some playing time. I watched him play and he was probably the 4th best player on the team. His biggest issue was he was trying to be fancy and do all these moves he couldn't do. He wasn't that fast or quick and for his size and age, he was a little overweight. As a result, he turned the ball over a lot. So when we trained, I taught him basic footwork, and fundamentals and taught him how to shoot. He hated those workouts and it showed in his facial expressions, body language and attitude. But eventually he had bought in.

WITHIN A MONTH, this kid was dominating games. He was the man. His team went to a tournament in Atlanta and saw a kid playing the style he and his parents wanted him to play. His parents were raving over a move that a kid in Atlanta did that had the crowd going wild. That's what they wanted him to learn. They were satisfied with his growth, but as plants still need watering, so does development. The gym we worked out in at the time was called Run-N-Shoot. It has multiple courts and different trainers had sessions on the different courts. I came in the gym one evening for workouts and saw him training with another trainer. So I continued to my court and one of the parents who's kid played with him, mentioned to me that his parents wanted him to do advanced dribble moves and I wasn't teaching them. First thing is that I teach according to the player level. Second, I teach fundamentals and basics. Footwork helps you to become a better dribble move player than learning a dribble move. To make sense of that, people talk about Kyrie Irving's handle all the time. If you watch Kyrie, he doesn't do a lot of fancy dribbles, he has fancy footwork and he's able to go down hill and handle the ball while his feet are consistently moving and able to get through any situation or window. That's what I teach. I have never seen a player with great footwork, that couldn't shoot or handle the ball to score.

ONE DAY A parent came in the gym and said, "your boy struggling." I went to a tournament to see him play and he was back on the bench pouting and upset. I wondered why and I asked the coach how he was doing. His coach says, "Coach, he's trying to do things that he can't do. Taking bad shots and not making smart plays." All I could think of was how a plant wilts when it's not being watered.

That was one of the biggest problems with grassroots basketball when I first started. Young players in the early stage of development, would start to blossom, leave for different soil that wasn't being watered. They didn't allow me to nourish the plant. My soil is fertile and organic. It's home grown. If you take a plant from fresh soil and replant it, if the soil isn't the same or similar, the color and strength of that plant will change. I could take any player and make them look good by putting them in position to be successful and developing them. But some didn't trust the process. They would go to other teams and the new coaches or team, would get that same player and expecting what they saw with me, and get a totally different player, not as good because what they saw was pre-mature. They still have to continue development.

I've always had an unorthodox method of developing players. When I started doing grassroots basketball, we didn't have tryouts like other teams. We were doing developmental training and we had a bunch of kids that weren't on teams for whatever reasons. Most teams didn't think they were good enough. So we started a team with what we had. Our first team was boys all different ages. When I was growing up, it wasn't 12's, 13's, 14's etc. It was 12 and under, 13-15 and 17 and under. Those were the age groups we played. We had boys ages 12 through 15 and they all played 15 and under. We were competitive but we lost a lot of games.

Still remembering the way I was developed, I used the same method to develop my players. On Saturday mornings, we had workouts for two hours. The first hour we would do fundamental development stuff. Since the training was only once a week, we would just spend time working on one thing. If it was ball handling, we would do that for the whole first hour. A variety of game types of drills that would translate when kids actually get in the game and play. For example, we would work on full court dribbling, finishing with a pass or a shot. But the concentration would be on the footwork of actually dribbling full court. When watching a player that just start playing for the first time, their feet are just as bad as their ball skills. So we would work on that first. If we were shooting, we would work on a lot of different ways and footwork to make shots off the catch. A lot of kids couldn't dribble well enough to create space and score off the dribble. So whatever the style of play we had to play, our workouts would be centered around the things we could do and work on them so we could do them well. #CC

The second hour, we would let the kids play pickup. I would recreate those Saturday mornings I played with the older guys growing up. I would let the kids pick their own teams, boys and girls mixed up together, all sizes and ages. Whoever you pick, that's your team. If you didn't get picked, you got next. You know today, the best kids want to play together. I wouldn't allow that. I would make them choose even teams. The games would be non stop, no calling fouls and I would just sit back and evaluate and observe. When I saw something, I would take a mental note and when they come off the floor, I would give them my advice and an alternative. I would tell them what I saw, and give them my solution and what I would have done, and other options. All it takes is to be right consistently, then you have their attention.

The games would be physical and fast with arguments, fouling and frustration. I loved it and so did they. They were looking forward to playing pickup and that's how they began to fall in love with the game. Faster than any training, they would begin to develop. With good experiences and instruction sharing, the players started to trust my teachings and it helped speed up the development process.. The parents could see it, others who know the kids and saw them play, would ask the parents, "who are you training with?" And word of mouth filled up the gym. We went from having two teams to about seven because people would start to see the improvement of the players.

Pickup allows the players to play freely and allows you to see what they can do best and the things they're comfortable doing. It also allows you to see how competitive they are and who they are individually as players. Once I evaluate each player, now I know their strengths and weaknesses. My focus becomes paying strictly attention to their strengths. That's the foundation of their confidence. You help a kid do what they do best and make it better, you get their trust and confidence goes up. The object of development is to get the best out of a player. Again, get the "best" out of a player. Not get their best out of their worst. The fastest way to that is strengthen the strengths. Allow them to do what they do best. From a Coaching perspective, you can't be afraid to adjust to what your players can bring to the table.

One of the biggest issues I have when consulting coaches is, trying to teach a coach who has been running the same system for years, and don't want to change it on the grass roots level. If you're coaching a middle school team, and you're running a whole bunch of plays and have a system, you're not helping your players out. This is the early development stage and what they learn now, is what they're going to be accustomed to. You have to not be afraid and adjust to what the players can do. There's no need to run plays if you don't have the players with the skills or IQ to get it done. They're just out there running what they've been taught and doing exactly what you say do. It's okay to teach them sets so they will become familiar with them. The same sets are used on every level, including inbounds plays. But a simple motion offense and teaching the basics such as the different types of screens, how to use, set and defend them. That's more important than any play. We all want to win, but don't sacrifice development for grassroots wins. That includes playing your players as well. Develop everyone on the team, and it will make your team stronger in the long run. It's a beautiful thing when you have a full team to trust you and you can trust them.

SKILL SETS

Recognizing a player's strength is, notifying their best skill. To become a highly skilled player, you have to train smart and train often. Training is a big part of development but it has to be training that will translate to your game. Studying the game is another way to better your skill set. A lot of kids today don't watch basketball. You have to watch the game to learn the game. Don't watch the moves and learn that, look at how the teams are competing, the movements the players make, the cuts, the fundamentals. Those things are as important as anything in the development process. You can be a great shooter, ball handler or passer, but if you don't know how to play the game, none of that matters.

The top 5 basketball skills categories, that I focus on to develop good competitive players are:

Shooting: Shooting is #1 because there is always a spot on a team for a shooter. The object of the game is to score the ball. Don't limit yourself to being a spot up shooter. Learn how to make all of the shot opportunities available. All shots have a different touch to them and footwork.

Footwork: You need proper footwork to be successful. Defensive and offensive footwork has to be on point. One of the biggest secrets to ball handling is footwork. The #1 thing to be a great scorer is also great footwork.

Passing: Passing is so invaluable. Take advantage of teaching or learning how to make every pass. Practice passing just as much as you practice shooting. Lack of passing is why press only work on the grassroots levels because kids don't know how to make fundamental passes. That also involves footwork.

Defense: A good defender has three things; heart, will and drive. The best defenders aren't always the best athletes. They just want to play it. Learn how to play defense by practicing the defensive movements of the game. Encourage playing defense whenever you're playing.

Dribbling: On someone's list, dribbling would probably be first. But I've found that, when a kid learns to dribble first, then that's what he's going to do the majority of the time. As soon as he feels pressure, dribbling will be the instinctive reaction. Passing is more important than dribbling. The ball moves faster and teams have better rhythm when the ball is moving. When working on ball handling, young kids should not spend all those hours on dribble moves. Players should work on the simple things that translate to the game.

"Shamefully, between the High School coach, scout and the collegiate coach, it's a rarity that the UNIQUE talent gets noticed! In order for that special talent to get noticed, it would take a coach or scout to have the ability to think outside of the BOX. Sadly enough the most common occupants this positions doesn't have the ability to have an original thought!

They are all used to mimicking each other to the degree of disgust. As a result, a 6'8 guard with 30 feet range on his jump shot, gets pegged as a forward/ Center and has to create a unique path to the pros where an ORIGINAL thinker would have saw and nurtured that talent much sooner."

- Coach Mike Bozeman

CHAPTER XXII :
Recruiting

FOR COLLEGE INTERESTED students, parents and coaches, there are a few things that we all should know about recruiting from a basketball stand point. This isn't about education at all. Just how recruiting works from the outside looking in. When we develop players, it's not for our team. It's to prepare them for whatever the next level is. In this case, we're going to look at the transition of being recruited as a high school athlete, to a college athlete.

Who you are as a person, matters most off the court, then on. Your attitude and character will either take you a long way, or it will leave you at home. College coaches are not interested in babysitting an immature kid. It's time to begin the growth and maturity process in High school. Growing up doesn't mean you can't have fun, it just means making good decisions, being responsible, organized, focused and dedicated to being a student and an athlete. That's a part of maturity. Show respect to people in general, teachers, the janitor or anyone of authority. College coaches talk to everyone you encounter. They want different perspectives because they know your family and friends will always make you out to be the best person. Watch what you put on social media. Social media is entertainment. Be careful with your content.

On the court, they watch your interactions with your coach and teammates. You see a lot of kids in grassroots basketball having attitudes during games and bad body language. All that gets noted. These are mental impressions you are leaving with someone who is interested in giving you a $150,000 scholarship. Be mind of your behavior at games. If you're locked in, you shouldn't have time to have attitudes anyway, it's too many things to think about in a game, then being upset over something that's not going to change the way you play. An attitude controls your feelings. If you have a negative attitude, how can you focus and perform well?

Aside from the emotional parts of life, what's attractive about your physical game that would make a coach want to recruit you? This is where your unique qualities come into play. One of the most important attributes of being recruited is being fundamentally sound. Playing basket- ball is a simple game. We complicate it by not teaching fundamentals and jump straight to advance training. Another recruitable attribute is being coachable. Be a great listener, we can see that you're listening by your posture, eye contact and when you get on the floor. Show that you know how to play. Play smart, and play hard. Be efficient. Take care of the ball and compete like it's your last game. Those are the most attractive attributes to a coach.

A lot of players have the same qualities. I can't stress this one thing enough, what separates you? This is why it's so important to find your game. Not the game your coach gave you, your trainer, your moms or pops, YOUR GAME! The things that you are comfortable doing. Your strengths, and the things you added to your game and made yours. If you cover these bases, you will increase your chances of getting into school. The level of school is dependent upon your work ethic and the height of your development.

Every kid and parent wants their kid in a D1 school. But realistically, every kid is not a D1 kid. There are differ- ent levels to D1, High Major, Mid Major and Low Major. Where you fall is solely on you. Being a High Major D1 player is a lifestyle. It definitely starts with your skill set. Most D1 high major kids are the master of some- thing. It also means that they work on their bodies, skills, have good grades and test scores. They also compete on a high level and show it when playing against players on the same level. Some kids take it for granted and because they're on a good team, they feel as if they should be a DI player. Don't fool yourselves or your parents. You can't cheat the process. It'll catch up at some point. So do the work now. You know how much work you're really putting in to get there. Everything is earned. Even if you make it, you have to prove that you belong. Scholarships are year to year. You have to earn it every year.

It takes a few more things to get to that level. Your high school team and Coach is one. Your Grassroots team is another. It is what it is, today these things will deter- mine and have 90% of the influence on your future as a basketball player. Let's discuss High School first. Most of the high major DI kids play on teams that play a competitive high school schedule. Whether it's a private school in a good conference or a independent school that plays a tough schedule, you have to compete against other top level players. Some independent schools and private schools play at a National level. A lot of schools have restrictions on travel and out of conference play. Most schools make it up by playing in holiday tournaments and showcases that host top ranked teams. Some public schools play in good conferences as well, but not many. It's a must when you pick a high school that you do your due diligence on the coach, the players on the team and the competition schedule. These things matter most. You need a coach who is going to help you grow and coach you up for those four years. You also need your coach to be active and contacting colleges and giving updates on your growth and progress. College Coaches like those updates.

Interview your potential coach. Find out his/her philosophy and how you fit in their system and what he will ask of you. Find out the goals for the players each year and in the future. Get a clear cut idea so you can know what your job is, going in. Find out what your role will be and how the coach will help you settle in to it. You should never go into this situation guessing and not knowing what's expected of you. Every player has a role.

Grassroots are a little different. You want to begin play- ing for an organization that has a commitment to development first. A team that's going to teach you the game and let you play it. Not handcuff you to their system. You need to be able to play freely and learn during the process. As you get better and start to see the development, your team should grow together and begin to play in more competitive events. If not, play on a team that plays on a high level against other top teams in top brackets. That's if you're a player on that level. Don't go team chasing to play on a top circuit and you don't get a chance to showcase your game. The purpose is to showcase your talent in front of the College scouts. Use the same process that I mentioned for high school coaches.

Do your due diligence, it's very important, especially on your grassroots team. Your grassroots team may be better than your high school team. More talent and more players get minutes. So you will really need to know where you fit in. College coaches that attend these games, have a schedule of games they've planned to see and a list of players they want to see. Most of the time, they are there to see players that they have on their radars, offered or want to take another look at. The games you see when there's a lot of Coaches watching, it's multiple players on both teams that they are there to support. Sometimes a new kid may jump out on their radars with consistent out- standing performances, that's how it works. But more times than not, they are watching players they're recruiting already, or have already offered.

Top High schools get more looks during the school year than spring and summer grassroots season. The NCAA recruiting calendar lasts over a 5 month period during the school year. Coaches can come to practices, workouts (open gym), and school games. Lot's of offers are given during this period. Then they follow up during the grassroots season to see more of the player. Playing time is tricky in all of these situations. Your expectations should be nothing given, everything earned.

Here's just a few things to think about during this process:

FRESHMAN: You're going to high school for the first time. It's a lot to learn about the game, from the speed to the strength of the game and the coaches system. It's a difficult transition for most. If you are good enough to play Varsity, but you're not playing significant minutes, put the pride to the side and ask the coach to play JV as well. It's a good part of development because most of the time, JV runs the same system as Varsity and those reps will help your learning curve. If you're not playing a lot in practice or in games, don't waste a whole season on the bench barely playing just because you're on the varsity team. It's not about the level of competition on JV either, it's about your learning curve and preparation for the varsity level.

Sophomore: This transition is a little better. Hopefully you remember what your freshman experience felt like, and you raise your level over the summer during the grassroots season. You should come back to school ready to compete for minutes. If you're in the same situation not playing significant minutes, play JV again to get your reps.

Junior: For me this is my target year. When I started grassroots basketball, I told my parents that it all matters in the eleventh grade. This is when everything we've talked about in this book comes to fruition. This is show and tell time. It's time to blast off as a player. Let the world know who you are. At the time of this writing, my girls grassroots team are all rising Juniors. Most have been with me between third and fifth grades. We are ahead of our goal. They all have a lot of interest. By eleventh grade, players should have an idea and ready to make a commitment after their last summer of grass- roots basketball.

Senior: Hopefully the burden of getting offers and commitments to schools are gone. Sign during the first sign- ing period. Get it over with so you can focus on getting better. This is the year you should be preparing for college. Your coach should be preparing you for college. You will receive your accolades, 1000 points, McDonalds Nominee and all the other things that you're interested in. You know the game now. Be a great leader to the young and usher them in. Show them how to do it. They're watching you. Set the example in practice, workouts, preparation and in games. Leave your mark.

The butterfly is leaving the cocoon. You're soon to be a college player. Your college coach should be receiving a more mature person from who they have been recruit- ing over the past year or two. Your body should be physically prepared. Your workout routine and study skills should be a habit. Your focus should carry over and leadership skills should still be intact regardless of your class. Keep being a student of the game and getting better. Development never stops.

Trust is the very first thing that has to happen in any process. All parties involved have to have trust in each other. Without trust, there is no belief. If you don't believe it, you won't have confidence. We know what confidence does for players, it's EVERYTHING!!

I want to take a look at the process for both coaches and players. This union is more important than a lot of us may think. Just like a relationship, you're going to have ups and downs and things are going to have to come together in order for things to be positive and work out. Positivity is the key to all confidence. #CC

Everyone has had a bad relationship. Whether it's at work, with a mate or Coach. We all have suffered a bad one. If the relationship is what you want, you will have to work it out. Nothing is perfect and it will always be something wrong. When a Coach and player don't see eye to eye, the first thing to do is find a common place. The Coach is the leader of the team, that's #1. So you have to deliver whatever it is that the coach asks of you. And #2, as a player, find out what the coach wants! That way you know going in what's expected of you. Communication is key!

Coaches:

ALL COACHES HAVE philosophies or systems and most are set in their ways. Coaches should first teach fundamentals and how to play the game both mentally and physically on the Grassroots level. You should be allowing the players on this level to play freely with a teachers (The Coach) guidance. Watch them closely and correct them on the fly. One thing you will find out is, who they are as players. They will show you their strengths and weak- nesses in free play or pickup. Now you can evaluate and build your team based off of what you have witnessed.

This will also test your evaluation skills, and i'm not talking about rankings. If you can't evaluate players, you should be working under a coach on the grassroots level that can, so you can learn to evaluate. Encouragement is also key to confidence. A lot of coaches yell and give what they call tough love to players. They're hard on kids, trying to make them tough. But tough love won't get all kids as far as instilling confidence in them. Being hard on a kid won't help them be- come mentally tough. How many kids have you seen respond or play good when parents and coaches are yelling at them? The kids who are more confident are usually the best players and having fun.

THE IMPORTANCE IS in the message, not the tone. You can get loud, be a passionate screamer, but the message is key. When a kid makes an effort mistake, instead of yelling "what in the world was that?" Try taking a more supportive approach and commend the kid for the effort, then correct him/her. Tell them what you saw and what they should do next time. This will trigger two things. one, it will reward the effort and kids respond and feel good when their hard work is appreciated. This will also prepare them for future coaches in high school and on higher levels. Coaches don't have time to coach effort. And two, it's a lesson being taught and by com- mending them first, now they are open to listen and not rebel. It's a mental game.

The way I approach development and preparing layers to get recruited is different from most. It sounds differ- ent but I teach players to win, I don't coach to win. It's two different things. Teaching to win is more individualized and detail oriented. Coaching to win is game planning and scouting. I teach my players how to figure those things out themselves on the grassroots level. Over the years it has been successful for our Lady Prime Basketball program at the development level. My goal from the beginning was to develop players into versa- tile, position less players that can and will be able to play for any coach. I think we are accomplishing that. I never wanted to be a head coach, because I love playing the player development role and the consultant role for coaches, players and parents. The work we put in does not go unnoticed. I received a call from one of the top women's basketball programs in the country. They're always in the top 5 every season with multiple National Championships. This phone call changed my life and has given me the stamp of approval in this field. I was offered an opportunity that I have never been offered be- fore. Instead of them calling about a particular player to recruit, they called and told me that the have been watching what I have been doing with my program, and they want me to send them a player who I believe could play for their team. I can choose who that player is. That's an open offer!

For me to make that decision on which player to choose could cause some confusion, but it won't. I am equipped as an evaluator and a developer. I have two seasons to see who puts in the work and is mature enough in the classroom and outside the classroom that they will rep- resent their family and finish out once they land at the school. Either way, all the players will land where they deserve, but this is a testimony that shows, regardless of what's being said around you, your work will not go unnoticed. You have control of your destiny, College awaits you.

Players/Parents:

A part of the process should be recruiting the coach. Just because a coach has interest in a player, doesn't mean the player has interest in the coach. On the grass- roots level, families should be seeking a coach that develops players through fundamentals and teaching them how to play the game. Not a coach that has a system and is strict to his guidelines and has kids playing one way, and that's his way.

This is an experimental stage for the coach and player. If it's not a coach who has played on a high level or a coach who is coaching their kid, most likely the coach is a novice as well and the coach and player will grow together over the years. This goes to former players as well. You can teach and develop, but being a coach has it's own process as well.

When picking a coach, talk to players/parents that's on the team. Watch a game and talk to the kid that doesn't play the most, and to the kids who are role players. Never talk to the Super star kids or their parents about their experiences unless you're on the same level. More than likely everything is Smooth sailing for them, unless the team is losing. Make sure to have an open mind and just listen. It would help you find out some things about the Coach and his philosophy. Then when you talk to the coach, you can match up the two sides.

Most Organization directors are the ones who give the winning pitch to get you in. They will sell you all they have to offer and more. That's not what you should buy, the Coach is who you will be playing for, and that's who you should pay the most attention to.

Remember it's no where you can go and will receive exactly what you want. You have to be willing to do your part and be all in. Sacrifices have to be made in order to start the road to greatness. Greatness does not waver. It's taking the lessons as they come, learn from them and keep on pushing and finding ways to get better. The most important part is to keep on getting better. Development never stops! #CC

One of the biggest challenges for athletes is understand- ing what buying in means. When you buy in, it's committing to the philosophy, to being a member of a team and doing whatever is asked of you. It's playing your role and doing your job because you believe in what you're being taught. Some players struggle with this be- cause of outside influences. If your coach is asking you to do ABC, and someone else is telling you, you should be doing XYZ, and you are doing AXBYCZ, then you're not buying in. Regardless of the situation, whether you think it's right or wrong for you, it's a lesson and will make you a better player regardless.

I hear a lot about how bad a coach is and how things aren't working. I think a lot of these relationships don't work because the due diligence hasn't been done and players aren't giving the situation a chance. It's no special system or way to play, that will guarantee a win. You have a coach who likes to play a certain way, and it will always be a challenge. A part of developing is figuring out how to make things work. Fitting in with others is a real thing. Regardless of what you expect, having the freedom to play and figure things out, or having the green light to take shots, there will always be structure that you have to conform too.

Trust is everything in sports development. Coaches have to trust the players and players have to trust the coach. It's key because of the time invested. Don't waste time worrying about the situation, spend that time on making the situation work. The Process doesn't produce fast results like a microwave. You can't just pop a player in and pop out an All American. It's a slow cook like a conventional oven. You get a better meal when you cook it slowly and let it take its time. This is the approach and thought process you have to have to get better in any situation. It's always a lesson in every opportunity and decision that you make. Embrace it, buy into it and make it work for you.

My first year in the NBA G-League, I was the 7th pick in the draft, to the Huntsville Flight. I had just left the New Jersey Nets of the NBA. I was sure to be a lock on the Nets after having a great Veterans Camp. Then one day, the Doctor comes to practice and that was the end of my time there. Once I got to the G-League, I was in great shape, and ready to play. The team had picked up some other players that came down from the NBA, and the Coaches put them in the starting lineup. I felt that I was the best player on the team, so I was all for proving it.

The system the coach had us running, wasn't my favorite, because I was used as a passer and a defender, when I was one of the best scorers on the team. I had to play my role if I wanted to play. So I defended and I passed the ball to the other scorers. I did my job so well that I got more time. With more time, came more touches. With more touches came more opportunities. I went from not starting, to leading my team in every statistical category. I made the situation work for me.

I've been around other Pros and I saw how they approached the game. I kept the mentality I saw from professional players and used it for me. I became a leader because of it. I manipulated the situation and it made us a better team, and it helped me rise above my previous judgement or perception the coach had of me. Thinking I was a limited substitute, and if anyone was comfortable with that, they were wrong. I didn't ask why I wasn't starting or complain about players getting more touches or more shots. I did my job until I was able to come for- ward and get what I deserved. I never settled and was never satisfied. I did my job that I was asked to do. I used the tool necessary, but had my whole toolbox on standby. When it was my time, I was ready.

CHAPTER XXIII:
Shooting & Ball Handling
"Make what's comfortable work"

I had to add this Chapter because one of my greatest skills is shooting. If there's anything about basketball that I can say it's no two are alike when shooting. Some won't agree with this, especially old school coaches and maybe some players, but there is no proper way to shoot. The elbow tuck, the break your wrist, the feet shoulder width apart and my all time favorite, the knee bend, does not work for everyone. It's cool when you're a child and someone is teaching you how to shoot and they condition you to believe that this is the correct way, it will work for you. But that's with any style of shooting. Basketball legend Rick Barry shot 90% from the free throw line for his entire 15 year career. His un- orthodox underhanded shooting style was not the norm.

How is that possible? It's an example of what works for you is for you. He worked at it and he found that it was a more comfortable shot for him. If you take a 7 year old kid and teach him to shoot with one hand or even teach a right handed kid to shoot with his left hand, that's what they will do. Your shooting style and form isn't what makes the ball go in.

In high school I shot an unbelievable field goal percent- age as a jump shooter. I shot 68% from the field. I was never taught to tuck my elbow, but the older guys did emphasize the follow through. But I learned that different shots took different touch. I couldn't shoot a spot up jump shot the same way that I shot a transition pull up. You have to factor in momentum. When I got to college, my coaches corrected my mechanics and I became a streaky shooter. My release didn't feel comfortable and my shot wasn't smooth anymore. It looked good, but I lost my stroke. That would play on my confidence and I would be off for multiple games. I still shot well, but not as good as I knew I could.

Not until i finished college, did i go back to what I knew and one reason for it was because I could shoot however I wanted. When I spent time in Boston, I was able to see Reggie Lewis. Reggie also had an unorthodox shooting style. He was the first player that I saw kick his leg out when he shot jump shots. Similar to my theory about different touch on a spot up shot opposed to a transition shot, Reggie taught me that when you're coming off screens or motion shots that kicking your leg out, will help you line up your body and continue shooting through the natural rhythm of your movement. I mastered that and it was another level of shooting that I have learned.

Learning that one thing from Reggie, made me hungrier to learn more about shooting. So I would go out and start taking all kinds of shots just to find a smooth stroke and rhythm to shooting. When I played in pick up games, I used to piss a lot of people off because I would take these crazy runners, and jumpers without setting my feet, left handed and right handed to see what I could come up with. I was practicing. Pickup games were the best practice and training for me. It allowed me to be creative in competitive games.

When Summer League would come around, I would shoot these crazy shots and consistently make them. I was an entertainer. People loved to come and see me play to see what I was going to do next. I wasn't afraid to try anything because that's how I practiced. I had a solution for everything offensively. I was unguardable. I could shoot mid range, threes and beyond the three. I even used to pull up from half court. I could score on four different levels.

This type of shooting is far beyond your typical mechanics. It's touch, a feel and a mental belief that everything you shoot is good. It also takes a lot of footwork. To be great at something, you have to do it over and over with purpose. First learn the footwork of every shot you want to take. Then find a shooting style that's comfortable for you. Next you have to practice shooting to keep the ball on line with the basket. Once you get that consistently, then you practice on a smooth stroke and learn how it feels when the ball goes in. Duplicate that feeling. You have to do this all over the court until it's like the back of your hand. Know the floor, know your spots and re- member the feel. That's what muscle memory is about. It's not just doing it over and over and over. You have to accomplish something while doing it over and over. It's why a lot of NBA players today can't shoot. It's more than repetition, it's a mental concentration that creates a shooter.

Shooting is more mental than anything. When I first started coaching girls, I had a team of 2nd, 3rd, 4th and 5th graders. Unbeknown, the team was far more advanced than any team it's age. So we added two kids that were in the 7th grade because we didn't have any bigs to play Center or forward and the lower grades played up to 7th grade level. We competed in 7th grade Nationals and finished 4th in that Grade bracket. We were really good. At practice one day, a new kid came in the gym and was a beginner. She was only 4th or 5th grade. She came in and saw how good the team was, started crying and didn't want to play. She did not want to try because she was a beginner and saw how skilled the other girls were. When she saw that it was girls her age that could actually play, she shut completely down.

She had no fundamentals at all, couldn't dribble shoot or anything. I told her moms to just sit on the side and let her watch and she could come back another day. They accepted the offer and stayed. They returned to the next practice and she participated. I mentioned that she couldn't play, so the times in drills when she had to handle the ball, she traveled, shot it on top of the backboard and the ball was just going all over the place when she would shoot. But, she loved to shoot.

Now this is why this story is important. The first thing I noticed and it's the majority of kids, is that she loved to shoot. Now when I say she loved to shoot, as soon as she caught the ball anywhere in half court, she would just hoist up a shot from anywhere. That's what she loved to do So I took the time to help her with her shot and I be- gan to call her "shooter." People thought that I was crazy. But, they didn't matter, she believed it. It got to a point when she would actually begin to make shots. This same year and actually a few months after she started playing, we were playing in a league and it was the Championship game. We were playing against one of the best teams in our age group for the Fall League Championship. This same kid that could not shoot made 5 three pointers in the biggest game of her life, at that time Mentally a seed was planted, she accepted it, and had the confidence and believed that she was a shooter. She became one. Fast forward to her High school years, she was the best shooter on her team and was who they looked for to make threes. All because it was planted in her and she believed it.

In all of this, it won't happen overnight. It's a level of commitment focus, drive and knowing how, that will make you a great shooter. The same way it's no one way to bowl, it's no one way to shoot. Make it work for you.

The Cheat Code Is Real

During the pandemic, we faced a very challenging time for High School basketball. Seasons were cancelled for public schools. Private schools had delays. Winter sports were scheduled to begin in the Spring and the Independent schools had a little more wiggle room to create a make shift season. We played under an independent schools umbrella. The school we were at before which was a National Powerhouse, cancelled all sports because of the pandemic. My coach at the time decided to move to this new school so we could continue to play and salvage whatever we could for a season.

More challenges arrived when it came to practicing and gym time for workouts. We had to have our high school practices twice a week in a shared gym full with trainers, players and other teams. You can imagine the dis- tractions and focus required to hold the players attention and to be able to teach. We played 5 regular season games, out of the five months time. The school that we all moved to, to play, did not support our efforts, and our experience was similar to an AAU season. We were all to persevere and make it through.

Locally, we played in a league that had around 16 teams from our area, playing in one location that did a great job of adhering to Covid protocols and created a safe place for our players to play. It had a lot of the top teams in the area participating, but I looked at it as am opportunity for another practice and scrimmage against other teams.

The way I wanted my kids to play was to create a system where each kid can play their game and make it work for everyone. I didn't want to tell kids to do A,B & C, when they're capable of doing D, E & F as well.

So the challenge was to teach them this style of play that involves a higher level of IQ. So we used the league to practice and get them to play this way.

In doing so, I had to tell the girls to put what people think to the side, and we will experiment and see what works while also learning how to play and increase our IQ. Although we want to win, this is our practice. So don't worry about your peers and what other teams are doing. Other independent teams were playing almost a full season because we didn't all under any county rules or restrictions. Our concerns came from our parents and caused us to cancel all of our travel dates. So this league came in handy.

We had a very successful experience in the league. We won games and lost. Few. We lost to a few teams that we shouldn't have lost to, and played some game closer the they should have been. With our talent, the criticism came and fingers were pointed at the coach and we were labels as underachievers. We should be better. But what they didn't know was that this was practice for us. I told my kids that I will take the blame because I can deal with it.

As the season drew closer to the end, we started to pre- pare for the Independent High School Nationals. Some of the top teams in the country were participants who were nationally ranked and we were the only team that wasn't ranked. This is what we prepared for and it was time to show and prove. We matched up against the #1 team in the country for our first game of the week. We only traveled with 8 players because of injuries and Covid. To play on this level in 3 back to back games, your bench is a key part of that. Two Senior starters did not travel, but from the beginning of my coaching experience, I never relied on my best players to carry my teams. I fought with two fist that were made up of 10 fingers. Each finger plays a roll in making a fist. That is how I view my teams. So if a player goes down, it's the next man up and nobody looks for the crutch.

We played the game and everything came together as planned. Our defense was stiff and offense was flowing. Everything we worked on in the league came together and we took down the #1 team in the country our way. No ranked players (rankings are someones opinion), unranked team, first time head coach, a school that didn't have any sports, a new team, only 5 games in 5 months and took down the #1 team in the country. The Cheat Code is real!

The CC 11 Keys of Development;

- Learn the basics & fundamentals

- Master the footwork of the game

- Play lots of pickup

- Evaluate each player

- Recognize their strengths

- Strengthen their strengths and develop the weaknesses

- Encourage and build confidence

- Preach being competitive daily

- Introduce a balance of comfort and discomfort

- Teach the basics of defense

- Have fun

CHEAT CODE KEYS

T RANSLATION IS ALSO recognizing a fit and making it work. It's not just skills and drills, it's also dialogue that helps by increasing their IQ and sharing experiences. Development is what everyone abuse by using the word "Process." Development is the "process" of going from A to Z. Being taught the basics, fundamentals and figuring out who you are as a player and building on that. It's understanding the game and how you fit in it. It's the experience of developing into.... in this case, a basketball player.

- Make it yours

- Imagination is everything

- Know what it feels like (brain muscle memory)

- Get it right your way. Figure it out.

- Make your skill set match your athleticism

- Master the fundamentals

- Discover who you are as a player

- Learn everything and master one

- Versatility is the goal, then be whatever a coach or team needs, whenever they need it

- Bring your tool that's needed, but travel with the full toolbox

- There is no better teacher than experience

- Having a point guard mindset at any position is an ad- vantage

- Manipulate the game

- Knowing your job and what you can consistently bring to the game

- Give it your all and be okay with that

- Your love for the game should be your motivation

- Footwork, footwork, footwork and more footwork!

About the Author

Lonnie Harrell, Father to Taylor Harrell, Author of "Cheat Code," Organization Director, High School Coach, AAU Coach and entrepreneur. I was born and raised in South East Washington, D.C. I began my basketball career at 14 years of age. That's when I began to play under the whistle. Before that, I was a football player at #11 Boys and Girls club in DC. I used to play basketball with my friends, but never on a team because football was our favorite sport and I wanted to be an NFL Quarterback. I never played middle School basketball and I only played one full year of High School basketball, my Senior Year.

After High School, I attended and played at Georgetown University. I transferred from Georgetown after my sophomore season and attended Northeastern University in Boston Massachusetts. Upon completion of college, I played in the ABA (pre NBA Draft), then I signed with the Orlando Magic (un-drafted), played in the CBA, USBL, International, New Jersey Nets, G League, the And 1 Mixtape tour then finished up Internationally.

Between High School and going to College, I have played so much basketball that shaped me into the player I was and the Coach that I am today. Along this journey, I have played for and learned from Hall of Fame coaches and hall of fame players. To name a few coaches; John Thompson, Larry Brown, Brian Hill, Byron Scott, Pat Riley, Dave Leitao, Eric Musselman, Terry Stotts,

George Karl and Darryl Dawkins. Players that i've played with; Alonzo Mourning, Allen Iverson, Patrick Ewing, Bay Bay Durham, Magic Johnson, Ray Allen, Penny Hardaway, Dennis Scott, Nick

Anderson, Baron Davis, Vince Carter, Kobe Bryant, Michael Jordan, Derek Anderson, Jamal Crawford and many more.

My basketball experience has been a fulfillment of gaining knowledge, sharing moments and learning from some of the greatest to ever be involved in the sport. All of the people named have influenced me on this journey. I've learned so much from so many people, and was still able to discover me. Today I share these lessons with kids and players around the country, and plant a seed to assist in the growth and development of players.

Lonnie Harrell

conKrete Playground 2021 ©